Sovereign DisCredit!

by

David Roche and Bob McKee

ISBN 978-1-4457-5976-0

The authors

David Roche is President and chief global strategist of Independent Strategy, a global investment consultancy based in London, Hong Kong and Zurich. He has worked in the investment business for over 30 years and was formerly global strategist for Morgan Stanley before founding Independent Strategy. He has been acclaimed for predicting the Fall of the Wall and the end of the Soviet era in the 1980s; the emergence of global disinflation in 1990s with purchasing power going from corporations to the people; and for forecasting the Asian financial crash of 1997-8. In 2006, he developed the theory of New Monetarism that predicted the global credit crunch. Irish, he lives in Hong Kong with his seven wild dogs.

Bob McKee is chief economist at Independent Strategy. He has worked in the investment business for decades and was formerly part of David Roche's global strategy team at Morgan Stanley. Like David, he is a regular contributor to business broadcasting including TV with CNBC, BBC, Bloomberg and others, as well as for various printed journals. He worked with David in developing the theory of New Monetarism and its prediction of the credit crunch. He is British and lives in London.

Contents

Preface

This book describes the next stage in the great credit-fuelled asset bubble that burst in 2007. Back then, we wrote *New Monetarism*, which explained why and how the credit bubble developed and forecast that it would burst, just as the crunch began.

We could not resist getting out another book to deal with the next stage of this crisis — a sovereign debt crisis that has no precedent in its magnitude and its global scope.

We'd like to thank everybody for their feedback over the past two years that inspired the ideas in this book, along with the efforts of other economists and investors in generating great new research to explain and confirm the nature of this upcoming crisis.

April 2010

Introduction

The next stage of the bursting of the great credit bubble engendered by the New Monetarism of the last two decades is with us. The private sector credit crunch is being overtaken by a global sovereign debt crisis. Sovereign debt will increasingly be discredited in financial markets.

Sovereign debt is normally deemed risk-free. It is the touchstone by which other riskier financial assets are priced. It forms the core of low-risk portfolios destined to fund real social needs like pensions or casualty and catastrophe insurance. It is the liquid asset that lies at the heart of current regulatory reforms to oblige banks to hold sovereign debt in proportion to their exposure to riskier assets and potentially illiquid short-term funding.

A repricing of sovereign debt as risky debt would be an earthquake for financial markets. It would blow a hole in the balance sheets of previously safe financial institutions. That would be a new chapter in the credit crisis. But it is a logical progression.

During this financial crisis, far from being a substitute for private sector deleveraging, which is only at an incipient stage, the state has piled on its own layers of debt. Leverage has never been higher (Figure 1).

Government dissaving in the form of structural primary budget deficits equivalent to 9-10% of GDP has been added to already inadequate levels of household savings. If over-indebtedness and

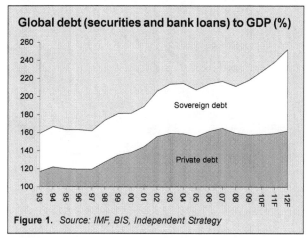

Figure 1. *Source: IMF, BIS, Independent Strategy*

lack of thrift were the causes of the credit crisis, the policy prescription has been akin to giving the dope fiend more dope. Over the decades, the expansion of US debt has delivered less and less in extra national output. In the 1960s, each dollar of new debt generated about 70c of dollar GDP. At the peak of New Monetarism in 2006, it delivered only 20c (Figure 2).

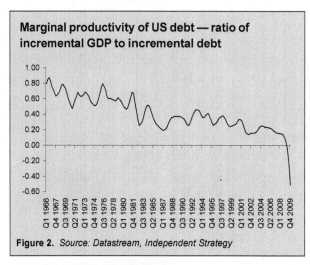

Marginal productivity of US debt — ratio of incremental GDP to incremental debt

Figure 2. *Source: Datastream, Independent Strategy*

By the end of this year, OECD sovereign debt will have exploded by two-thirds from 44% of GDP in 2006 to 71%. In the G7 economies, the explosion is even worse. According to the latest estimates of the IMF[1], G7 sovereign debt as a share of GDP has reached a 60-year high, at more than 112%, and is set to surpass that over the next few years (Figure 3).

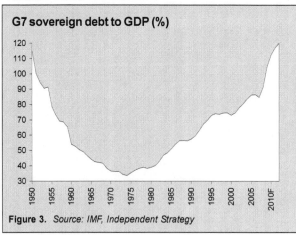

G7 sovereign debt to GDP (%)

Figure 3. *Source: IMF, Independent Strategy*

According to the Bank of International Settlements[2], it would take fiscal tightening of 8-10% of GDP in the US, the UK and Japan every year for the next five years to return debt levels to where they were in 2007 (Figure 4).

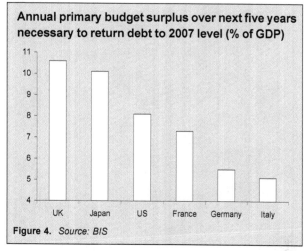

Annual primary budget surplus over next five years necessary to return debt to 2007 level (% of GDP)

Figure 4. *Source: BIS*

Some say that a temporary increase in sovereign debt always happens after a credit crisis. Research by US economists Carmen Reinhart and Kenneth Rogoff shows that sovereign debt rises by an average of over 86% in real terms within three years after a financial crisis[3].

But this credit crisis is like no other. Our own calculations show that the budget deficits of crisis-struck countries are now equal to over 25% of global savings and 50% of savings within the OECD. And the increase in debt ratios is on a different scale because it simultaneously affects all the major rich economies, not just one or two small ones. Indeed, countries with high deficits and debts now account for 40% of global GDP compared to just 5% in previous debt crises[4].

Other studies by the IMF[5] and by Reinhart and Rogoff[5] also show that there exists a tipping point — when sovereign debt breaches 60-90% of GDP — beyond which the impact of more state spending is to reduce

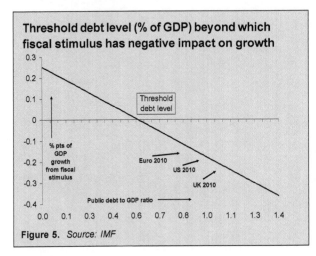

Figure 5. *Source: IMF*

growth and even to make the economy shrink (Figure 5). Sovereign debt is already (or is set to rise) above such a tipping point in the US, the UK, and the Eurozone. It is already more than twice that level in Japan.

This means rich countries will lack a dynamic core to help them grow their way out of their debt spiral by boosting GDP. Indeed, if growth falls below the yields on their bonds, these countries will become sovereign black holes in the universe of credit, with uncontrollable upwardly spiralling debt levels.

It has been possible in the past for countries to run unsustainable fiscal arithmetic for lengthy periods. Italy did so for eons. Japan has been at it for a decade. But to achieve that, a country must have high domestic savings that citizens want to keep at home in 'safe' investments. The vast majority of government debt must be owned by domestic investors, not by foreigners. And it needs a fat excess of gross domestic savings over investment needs, which yields a current account surplus. This keeps the currency strong and makes low domestic returns look good relative to those of foreign assets.

None of the major credit crisis-stricken states has any of these strengths today. Even Japan now has a household savings rate below the inadequate level of the US. None can fund their debts and deficits domestically on a durable basis. They will all have to sate their appetite for funding at the same trough of international savings, which will re-price them to reflect their true nature as risky assets. This will happen as soon as central banks stop monetising government debt by buying their bonds and when domestic savers take fright.

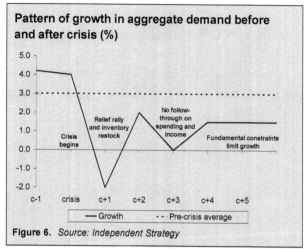

Figure 6. *Source: Independent Strategy*

Creating new sovereign borrowing to finance another thriftless consumer binge and more asset bubbles is no way to achieve sustainable growth. Unless immediately addressed, the excess of sovereign debt will be the next chapter in the credit crisis.

At best, the cost of debt will rise sharply and economic growth will be weak as the quality of sovereign debt deteriorates (Figure 6). At worst, there could be a series of debt crises and defaults like Argentina or Greece, but next time in larger economies. Such an event would risk plunging the world back into recession or worse, depression.

The cost of all capital will rise, as most forms of it are priced off sovereign debt on the assumption that this base is risk-free. OECD economies will expand more slowly as booming sovereign debt 'crowds out' the private sector from accessing the available savings it needs in order for the economy to grow.

Longer term, there will be some potential silver linings that could emerge from the other side of this debt crisis. The fiscal war in the Eurozone will mean that Germany will take the initiative, imposing prudent policies throughout the monetary union.

INTRODUCTION

A Japanese sovereign debt shock could jolt politicians into implementing policies that could rejuvenate an ageing Japan.

And the collapse of China's state-sponsored credit bubble could mark the point for a middle-class consumer revolution to become the dominant driver of its economy.

1. IMF *Global Financial Stability Report*, April 2010

2. *The future of public debt: prospects and implications*, Bank of International Settlements, February 2010

3. Carmen Reinhart and Kenneth Rogoff, *This time is different, a panoramic view of eight centuries of financial crisis,* April 2008

4. Wlllem Buiter, Citibank

5. IMF *World Economic Outlook,* April 2009, p128

6. Carmen Reinhart and Kenneth Rogoff, *Growth in a time of debt*, January 2010

CHAPTER ONE

Asset bubbles and New Monetarism

"The housing bubble is not a reflection of what we did at the Fed as it is a global phenomenon; it is a market phenomenon that has no real fundamental economic consequences". Alan Greenspan, November 2007

The common cause of all financial bubbles and their consequent bursting is an underpriced and excessive supply of credit. According to seminal research at the Bank of International Settlements[1], when credit growth is significantly above trend, it is a very good indicator of financial or economic crises to come (Figure 7). BIS researchers found that when credit growth is 4-5 percentage points above trend or asset prices are 40-50% above trend, this predicted nearly 80% of crises within a time horizon of one to three years.

It makes sense that too much money chasing too few assets is the *Ursprung* of all financial crises. This was the key theme of our earlier book, *New Monetarism*. In

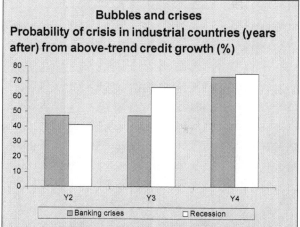

Bubbles and crises
Probability of crisis in industrial countries (years after) from above-trend credit growth (%)

Legend: ■ Banking crises □ Recession

BIS researchers, Borio and Lowe, looked at the long-term relationship between credit growth in the G10 economies and the movement of asset prices. They found that there were 38 crisis episodes between 1970 and 1999 spread over 27 countries. They found that when credit as a % of GDP grew to 4-5% points above trend, it was followed by some form of financial crisis on nearly 80% of occasions within one year. When several factors are combined (credit, asset prices and the exchange-rate), the probability of a crisis (either banking or economic) was still around 40% two years out and around 70% four years out.

Figure 7. *Source: BIS*

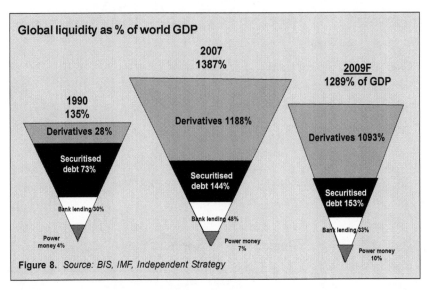

Global liquidity as % of world GDP

2007
1387%

2009F
1289% of GDP

1990
135%

Derivatives 28%

Derivatives 1188%

Derivatives 1093%

Securitised
debt 73%

Securitised
debt 144%

Securitised
debt 153%

Bank lending 30%

Bank lending 48%

Bank lending 33%

Power
money 4%

Power money
7%

Power money
10%

Figure 8. *Source: BIS, IMF, Independent Strategy*

that book, we argued that a huge inverted pyramid of liquidity had mush-roomed over 25 years to 2007 (Figure 8).

We first introduced the idea of monitoring monetary liquidity by measuring total credit (not just bank credit) using our liquidity pyramid. This was because traditional measures of liquidity only captured the liability (deposit) side of the banking system and not bank loans (assets) or loans made outside the banking system. If a banking system grew or shrank its loans relative to its deposits, the event would not be captured. Yet many credit bubbles (including the 2007-2010 credit crisis) have been financed by banks over-lending relative to their deposits. This so-called funding gap made the banks increasingly dependent on more volatile sources of finance.

Moreover, traditional measures didn't include all the credit and liquidity created outside the banking sector, as in securitised debt and derivative markets. Our liquidity pyramid concept expanded observed liquidity from one year to more than 12 years of annual global GDP. But it is still only a proxy for monetary liquidity because other sources, such as net household worth, are not fully represented.

Every credit boom is the same and different. A country viewed from an airplane at 30,000 feet looks the same as any other, but differs when lived in. Credit crises rhyme, but do not precisely repeat themselves. The current credit bubble and bust is no exception. Ironically, it was caused by disinflation — a phenomenon that lasted two decades. Disinflation was the result of sane central bankers conquering inflation by monetary means, starting with Paul Volcker at the Fed in the early 1980s.

As inflation fell year after year, the value of assets rose. This was for a very simple reason. The value of an asset is a function of its future earnings. Low inflation makes the asset worth more because its future earnings have more value today since they are no longer eroded by high inflation tomorrow.

Disinflation meant another thing too. It meant that it cost less to borrow — not only in nominal terms, but also in real terms. The decline in the cost of debt went on for the twin decades of disinflation (Figure 9). Now if asset prices rise continuously, making you richer while you sleep, why would you save? Why would you not even spend some of your wealth in order to boost your living standards a little beyond what your job would let you afford? Indeed, why would you not borrow to invest and consume more since it was costing you less and less to do so? This was the long process of replacing thrift by

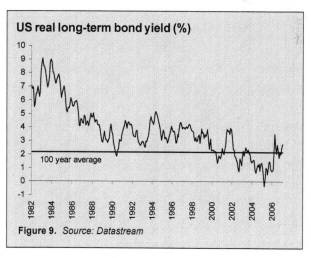

Figure 9. *Source: Datastream*

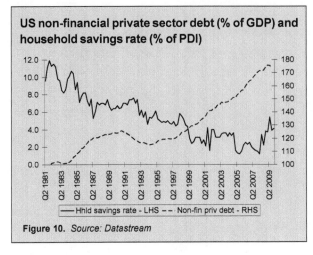

US non-financial private sector debt (% of GDP) and household savings rate (% of PDI)

Hhld savings rate - LHS — Non-fin priv debt - RHS

Figure 10. *Source: Datastream*

leverage that characterised the dark side of the otherwise unqualified virtues of the disinflationary decades (Figure 10).

Disinflation was not only the result of central bankers starting to target low inflation as a priority for monetary policy. A second force was the collapse of communism, which radically increased the global supply of skilled and cheap labour and, by raising these workers' living standards, created new (emerging) markets for their output.

A complementary force was globalisation that empowered producers of cheap things, like China, to sell their wares to rich folk without too much interference from protectionist tariffs or quotas. Simultaneously, the internet created competition in consumer markets and so shifted pricing power away from producers to the people. The internet also made it easier for companies to manage global supply chains more efficiently.

And finally, governments acted to empower markets rather than strangle them and also limit their own spending and deficits to some degree (although not nearly as great a shrinkage of the state as they laid claim to).

It was only in the second half of the disinflationary period that new forms of credit began to appear which met the appetite for new forms of borrowing created by disinflation itself. Financial players, increasingly sure of cheap money, began to introduce financial instruments, such as derivatives and securitised debt, that created liquidity independently of the central bank.

So central bank power money and bank lending became a smaller and smaller part of global liquidity — as expressed in our liquidity pyramid (Figure 11).

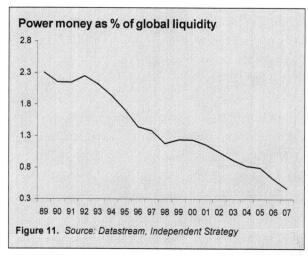

Figure 11. *Source: Datastream, Independent Strategy*

In other words, central banks lost control of the credit creation process. Previously, commercial banks could only lend out as much money as the central bank printed, for as many times as the reserves they were obliged to keep against deposits and loans would allow them.

By the end of the disinflationary period, credit was being created without any reference to central bank money, principally though the use of securitised debt. Securitised debt allowed banks to make a loan, repackage it and resell it. Banks made profit on the trade rather than holding the loan. Such transactions used up little of the banks' capital in precautionary reserves because the loans were shifted off the banks' books a nano-second after they were made.

Derivatives, such as credit default swaps (CDS) and interest-rate swaps, allowed banks to insure their loans against default (or changes of interest rates) with high-grade counterparties. In the case of a CDS, the risk of a bad loan disappeared and was replaced by the default risk of a 'good quality' counterparty to the CDS trade — the writer of insurance. This reduced the need to make reserves, which allowed the bank to lend more. In the end, the good quality counterparty turned out to be not so good after all (namely AIG, which at one point was writing 80% of CDS insurance).

Disinflation meant that price inflation in goods and services trended down. Not so for the prices of financial assets; they began to soar, as money got cheaper and more plentiful. There was little measured inflation in the shops, but for financial assets there was plenty.

Like all credit bubbles, it could only end in tears. Eventually, in mid-2007, the bubble burst; starting in the 'sub-prime' mortgage world, spreading to all forms of securitised debt and their derivatives and eventually destroying the assets and capital structure of the global financial system. Financial collapse led onto economic slump and the Great Recession.

Credit crunches are the result of credit bubbles — one breeds the other. The psychological driver of all bubbles is 'mania'. There is a strong human proclivity to act irrationally *en masse*, which is why the hypothesis underlying the theory of efficient markets is flawed from the outset. The shoaling phenomena can create a fad or fashion that will create mass demand for a product or service. If this causes its price to rise enough, it can become a bubble. It becomes a bubble if the price rises to a level greater than the object's sustainable economic value.

The sustainable economic value for an investable asset is simply the present value of the object's future income stream — real or imputed. For a machine, it's the profit it earns, for a house, it's rent.

Bubbles happen in consumer products too. People shoaled to buy limited edition *Tamagochi* electronic baby 'pets' for $1000; they waited five years and paid $50,000 to receive their orders for Hermes' *le Kelly Bag* in crocodile skin; and they queued all night to procure, by eating a burger, McDonalds' latest plastic figurines.

All were consumer product bubbles. Consumer product bubbles cause less damage than financial asset bubbles because they involve a mania about discrete products usually with very wide ownership distribution, representing a small part of what households buy and own. This is unlike the post-bubble distribution of bad debts and dud assets, representing a significant proportion of bank capital, credit and GDP, and which was concentrated in relatively few financial institutions.

Consumer product bubbles absorb relatively little direct borrowing leverage. There is no reason why unborrowed resources should not be irrationally concentrated on possessing an object (or service), causing its price to rise. The key point is that same shoaling psychology lies behind both forms of bubbles; credit is not always the driver. Indeed, it almost never is in consumer product bubbles.

All bubbles, whether they use leverage or not, are economically damaging. They misallocate resources, devoting too much to producing the object of the mania and not enough of other things. Once the bubble bursts, the aftermath is an overhang of excess capacity (malinvestment) and bad debts in the bubble product sector that have to be worked off. In the case of financial asset bubbles, this workout can depress aggregate demand and output for a considerable period.

The ultimate damage caused by (bursting) asset bubbles to the economy is proportionate to the degree that they are financed with credit. For the same asset bubble, economic damage will be greater if leverage is bigger and vice versa. This is because when the bubble asset price falls, the value of the debt used to finance it does not.

Take an example. A bubble asset's price is $100 and then falls to $60 when the bubble bursts. If no leverage was used to buy it, net worth has been reduced by $40 (40%). If leverage of $20 and net worth of $80 was used to buy the asset initially, when the asset price falls by $40, all the reduction in value must be absorbed by net worth, but leverage is unaltered. So net worth has dropped to $40 from $80. It's the same reduction of $40, but it's a 50% fall in net worth.

So the more leverage there is, the smaller will be the cushion of net worth to absorb losses. Once net worth is wiped out, there is no reason for the owner of the asset to honour loans. Credit default follows. This is how

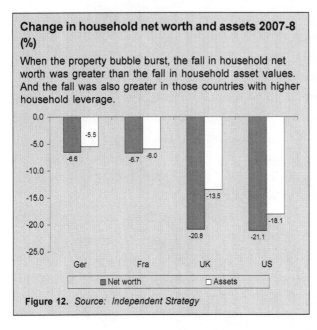

Change in household net worth and assets 2007-8 (%)

When the property bubble burst, the fall in household net worth was greater than the fall in household asset values. And the fall was also greater in those countries with higher household leverage.

Figure 12. *Source: Independent Strategy*

leverage increases the economic damage of bursting asset bubbles; it magnifies wealth destruction and credit losses.

Depending on the degree of leverage in the economy and the involvement of credit intermediaries in financing the mania, bursting bubbles will cause bankruptcies, credit contraction, wealth destruction and loss of jobs. These deepen and spread the economic cost (Figure 12). At the extreme, debt deflation can occur.

The level of debt that is relevant is unrelated to credit used to invest in the bubble asset. It is the existing aggregate leverage of the investor that counts, not the marginal amount of debt used to buy the asset. In the leveraged example, the damage to net worth from a $40 fall in the value of the bubble asset is the same dollar loss of net worth whether the debt of $20 was incurred to buy the bubble asset or a non-bubble asset. But the $20 of borrowing increases the proportion of net worth which is lost when asset prices decline above the loss that would have been incurred without leverage.

In other words, leverage will always magnify wealth destruction and economic damage from falling prices of bubble assets, irrespective of whether the borrowings were made to invest in the bubble asset or not. It is the overall leverage of balance sheets that determines how much the hit from falling asset prices will be magnified in wealth destruction and economic damage.

This is confirmed empirically by a study made by IMF researchers of 40 emerging economies during the financial crisis of the last two years[2]. They found that the extent of leverage in an economy explained most of the differences in damage to real GDP growth — in other words, countries with the greater leverage suffered the most.

This is relevant because the stock of global debt has not contracted since the credit crisis began either as an amount or relative to GDP. In fact, leverage has risen dramatically due to government borrowing.

Moreover, this credit bubble was no ordinary one. A credit bubble happens when excessive, often underpriced, capital inflates specific asset prices beyond what is economically reasonable or sustainable. A bubble is a relatively localised event where the price chart sticks up like a sore thumb from the surrounding financial landscape.

However, if excessive liquidity produces generalised asset price inflation over a prolonged period, the landscape itself alters. The tide of liquidity then lifts all economic boats (asset prices, wealth, demand, output and incomes) and becomes embedded in the warp and woof of the economy, creating an artificial level of well-being that is unmatched by improvements in productivity.

An economic reef is so-called because the excesses remain hidden below the surface of the flood of liquidity and leverage for as long as the boom times last (Figure 13). When liquidity finally subsides and the economic ship founders upon the reef, generalised deleveraging and increased risk aversion will drive the process of adjustment to a lower economic plane with an inevitable sustained reduction in GDP. This is essentially the dilemma facing the US economy and not a few European ones. Japan had to face it 15 years ago and failed to come up with policies that prevented its economic decline.

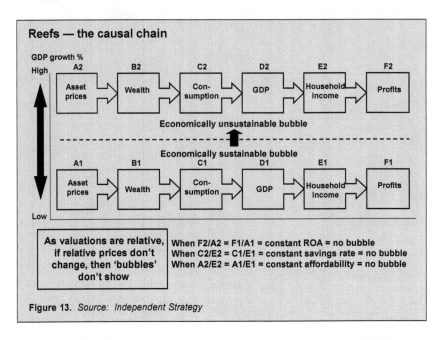

Figure 13. *Source: Independent Strategy*

It has been argued that the US economy outpaced 'sclerotic old' Europe for the last ten years of the disinflationary period because it had higher labour productivity. But if that productivity superiority were based on unsustainable growth produced by an economic reef (or super bubble), then the US productivity miracle never existed (Figure 14). The credit crunch suggested just that. In this sense, monetary policy that ignores bubbles or even promotes them will eventually be damaging to an economy.

To understand the crucial role of policy, let us dissect the credit flows currently driving asset prices. First, take the Fed. The Fed buys assets and creates money to do so. This money is paid to the seller of the asset. It shows up on the Fed's balance sheet on the liability side as either notes or coins in circulation or liquid reserves of the banking system.

This is an increase in Fed leverage, which is best measured by comparing the Fed's balance sheet to GDP rather than the ratio of equity to other liabilities. The Fed's balance sheet currently stands at over $2trn, or nearly 16% of GDP, compared to just $800bn, or 5% of GDP, in 2007. Increased leverage has been used by the Fed to sustain asset prices, because if the Fed were not a buyer, the prices would be lower.

Let us now assume that the sellers of the assets to the Fed are commercial banks and insurance companies. They have now got cash. What do they do with it? The banks, being loath to lend to risky private borrowers, might buy treasuries. This perpetuates low yields and finances government leverage directly or indirectly. It therefore perpetuates a bubble — this time in treasuries. The insurance companies might choose to increase their equity exposure, adding to the bubble in that asset category.

It is the increase in Fed leverage (buying an asset and printing money) in a manner that expands its balance sheet relative to both GDP and its own capital that lies at the base of this process. Thus, it is inaccurate to describe the asset bubble to which it contributes as being of the unleveraged variety just because the actual investors in the bubble assets (treasuries and equities) did not themselves necessarily have to borrow the money to do so.

Let us extend the range of possibilities. Suppose the proceeds from the Fed liquidity injection were lent to a portfolio manager who might invest it in expectation of a higher-return asset domestically, or exchange the dollars for an appre-

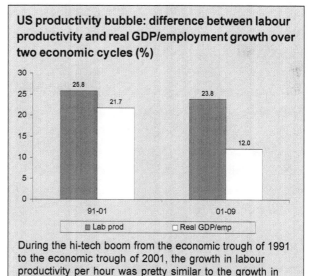

US productivity bubble: difference between labour productivity and real GDP/employment growth over two economic cycles (%)

During the hi-tech boom from the economic trough of 1991 to the economic trough of 2001, the growth in labour productivity per hour was pretty similar to the growth in real GDP per employee. In the financial credit boom from the trough of 2001 to the trough of 2009, labour productivity was almost double that of real GDP per employee growth — a bubble not seen since the 1970s.

Figure 14. *Source: OECD, Independent Strategy*

ciating foreign currency. That is a carry trade. It is entirely credit driven; borrowed dollars at low interest rates are invested in higher-yielding or higher (expected) return assets, domestically and abroad. As the carry trade is a major driver of global equity, debt and commodity price bubbles, it is false to state that these bubbles are unleveraged.

Finally, take the US government's role. It engaged in massive borrowing that increased the public sector debt to GDP ratio. The proceeds of these borrowings were distributed throughout the economy through transfers and asset purchases by the US Treasury. Transfers sustain household purchasing power. This generates demand for goods and services. But it is the household balance sheet effect that interests us. It reduces the incentive for households to deleverage and increases their demand for assets.

Furthermore, it is a multi-stage process. Every investment made with the Fed's cash injection leaves some seller of the asset with a new bank deposit which, if not lent by the bank to the 'real' economy, is likely to be used for further financial investments, pushing asset prices higher again — and so on and so on.

Policy thus contributes to sustaining the imbalance of excess consumption and inadequate household thrift, while adding a high public dissaving ratio of its own. This is the direct result of increased government leverage. It is hard to argue that such policies do not seek to sustain old bubbles as well as create new ones. The government's ability to do so by issuing debt also makes a nonsense of the claim that the current bubble is of the creditless variety.

Of course, leverage to inflate bubbles is not the same if it is the government rather than the private sector that does the borrowing, because government is less likely to default outright when asset bubbles deflate. This limits the contagion effect of bankruptcies and debt defaults transmitted via the financial system.

But the leveraged decline in the economy's net worth is still the same, irrespective of who does the borrowing. If government is the debtor, the loss of economic net worth incurred when bubbles deflate will ultimately be fiscalised (shown as a loss in the budget) and made up by increased taxation. Increased taxation results in less GDP growth and wealth creation. So the pain of collapsing asset bubbles, depending on whether the asset bubble is financed by the state or the private sector, may be processed differently by the economy and over a different time span. But the pain is still there; the piper has to be paid!

The theory of harmless bubbles is thus flawed in logic and in observation. It is, at best, a subconscious exculpation of central bank and government policies from the responsibility of creating current asset bubbles or for the damage that their inevitable collapse will do. As such, it adds to the long list of evidence that official policy nearly everywhere is being conditioned by denial of psycho-economic proportions.

The economic damage and asset price deflation experienced when the current asset bubble bursts will be greater because the level of leverage involved now is greater and the policy options to deal with any fallout are all but exhausted. So the next stage in the credit crisis will be the sovereign debt crisis.

1. Claudio Borio and Philip Lowe, *Asset prices, financial and monetary stability, exploring the nexus*, BIS working paper No. 114, July 2002

2. Michael Bordo, *When bubbles burst,* IMF, WEO, April 2003

CHAPTER TWO

The ultimate and the proximate

"Stronger regulation and supervision aimed at problems with under-writing practices and lenders' risk management would have been a more effective and surgical approach to constraining the housing bubble than a general increase in interest rates." Ben Bernanke, current Chairman of the Federal Reserve, January 2010

To cure any credit crisis two things need to happen: bubble asset prices must fall and those who have excessive debt (home owners, banks and governments) must deleverage. When that happens a 'natural' creditless recovery can take place.

But deleveraging of debt has not taken place in any significant way in the major economies since the credit crunch began. During the recession in the US, the ratio of non-financial private sector debt (businesses and households) to net worth continued to rise. The ratio remains well above pre-crisis levels. Major reductions in household debt have only just started on the long road down. The business sector also has yet to deleverage significantly.

By definition, the problem of asset bubbles can only be resolved by returning asset prices to a normal level, as discussed in the previous chapter. When asset bubbles burst, asset prices must find their own level in the market place. At that point, they often look cheap. But why market prices? Because the only known price is a market price. All other prices are opinions of interested parties (e.g. bankers and politicians) and are to be mistrusted.

There are always sufficient stocks of wealth to buy assets at some new lower level of market prices, which may indeed reflect under-valuation relative to their long-term earnings potential.

Let us set up a simple example, using the current credit crunch and the economic recession it caused. US household net worth at the nadir of the credit crisis fell by 20% and is currently still 10% below pre-crisis levels. During the recession, US wage income for those with a job rose 2%, while unemployment jumped to around 10%. So the total loss of household work-related earnings was around 8%. In other words, 80% of household wealth (more of corporate wealth) and 92% of household earnings power was still intact even at the worst moment of the credit crisis.

It follows that if the price of assets were to decline by more than 20%, they would be cheap in terms of the household wealth that could be used to invest in them. Similarly, if the prices of goods and services were to fall by more than the 8% fall in aggregate income, the real purchasing power of income would encourage people to buy again.

This shows that credit crises contain the mechanism (albeit painful) by which they are succeeded by creditless economic recoveries. This happens because the real purchasing power of remaining wealth and income rises compared to the prices of what can be invested in or consumed. But for that to happen, market mechanisms must be allowed to function. Indeed, under-valuation is the hair trigger that fires the economic cycle anew. Human greed and animal instincts (fear today and confidence tomorrow) are constants and come into play when that trigger price level is reached.

But in the course of doing so, much of the credit used to invest in the bubble assets will become 'bad'. Loans will be priced higher than many assets are worth. Therefore loans will be unserviced by equity holders in those assets, once their equity is wiped out. So those loans will have to be devalued against creditor capital.

Any measures that impede this process will result in: first, asset prices sticking at unrealistic levels; and second, bad loans being disguised as good loans on the balance sheets of creditors and debtors. The former will prevent the assets being cleared (sold off) by the lender in the market. This can prolong the life of 'zombie' assets and corporations (insolvent but still in business — the living dead of the corporate world!). This will leave lenders with uncleansed balance sheets that will impede their role in the future as efficient intermediaries between borrowers and savers.

Before the credit crisis, the household sector and much of the investment community in the US and Europe had been overleveraged. So asset prices had to fall. But that has not been allowed to happen to anything like the degree that markets would have dictated.

Instead, the US authorities have boosted lending to borrowers through the government mortgage agencies (Fannie Mae and Freddie Mac) and the Federal Housing Loan Board to sustain house prices artificially. The Fed has bought $1.25trn of mortgage-backed securities and $160bn of agency debt. The Fed and Treasury have also injected liquidity into financial institutions so as to sustain price dissimulation, by offering loans in return for mortgage-backed securities and securitised loans as collateral. They have tried to avoid home owner defaults by changing (violating) lending contracts.

Finally, the authorities have shifted the risk of investment from the markets to the state through loan guarantees and *de facto* nationalisation of the so-called government sponsored enterprises (GSEs), which currently account for most of US new mortgage lending. Capitalism knows no other way to price capital except by measuring and assuming risk. But if the state assumes the risk, capitalism has no yardstick by which to price investment.

The recipe for state and central bank intervention without distorting investment and keeping sovereign risk to a minimum was available. It had been written with the ink of experience. The US Savings and Loans crisis in the later 1980s and early 1990s had provided a draft, written over several hesitant stages. Then the Swedish banking crisis refined it a few years later. And the formula was applied successfully in the Asian crisis in the latter half of the 1990s.

The process is very simple (Figure 15). It falls into two parts: a solvency procedure and the maintenance of financial system stability. Take solvency first. Asset prices attached to non-performing loans are written down to market values. For creditors (e.g. banks), loans are written down by the reduction in the value of the assets they finance. Both repossessed assets and non-performing loans are then liquidated (the latter sometimes to asset management corporations).

Bank shareholders and creditors (after equity is wiped out) suffer the same (net) haircut as the loans. Where this makes banks insolvent, they are recapitalised, either by issuing capital in the market, or if that's infeasible, by the state. The recapitalised banks, where nationalised, are subsequently sold off.

This is a solvency procedure and is the responsibility of the state. It is driven by a mandatory audit procedure of all financial institutions that are critical to system stability, but deemed to be at risk.

As for financial systemic stability, the central bank is responsible. It can inject liquidity so that no entity that could cause the financial system to fail does so. So it can maintain functioning financial markets and provide accommodative monetary policy. But the central bank should have no responsibility for the solvency procedure.

What this achieves is a very thorough cleansing of financial intermediaries' balance sheets so that they can rapidly start lending again. And it does so while keeping the financial system on a fairly even keel. The separation of responsibilities dealing with solvency and financial system stability ensures two key things: one is that both jobs get done in parallel and the second is that one job does not interfere with the other.

Assume for a moment that the entire process was to be left to the central bank. To maintain system stability, it would at once be injecting liquidity into the same banks that it would be asking to devalue their loan books and so destroy shareholders' investments. Funds being fungible, and human

The accommodating and the strict approaches

The World Bank studied 30 years of systemic banking crises across 94 countries and near misses (or so-called borderline crises) that hit 44 nations (see World Bank discussion paper, *Managing the real and fiscal costs of banking crises*, January 2002). It found that there were two broad approaches to dealing with banking crises. The first was 'accommodating' involving measures of liquidity support to banks; guarantees to depositors and creditors of financial institutions; regulatory tolerance of violations of bank solvency and capital ratio rules; and debtor support schemes. The second was called 'sticking to the rules' where banks had to keep to recapitalisation regulations and there were no bailouts of creditors.

Japan adopted the accommodating approach in the 1996 rescue of Japan's zombie banks. It spent some 12% of Japan's GDP on loan losses, bank recapitalisations and depositor protection. The Japanese economy remained in the doldrums. In the US Savings & Loans crisis, both the accommodating and the strict rules approaches were adopted at different times. At first, the authorities tried to fund failing banks with credit insurance. However, the problem was so great that eventually Congress set up a new resolution fund that audited, losses and sold off assets or recapitalised. It cost the US taxpayer about $125-150bn, or 3% of annual economic output (see *The cost of the savings and loans crisis: truth and consequences*, FDIC Banking Review, December 2000).

In the early 1990s Swedish banking crisis, the authorities opted for the strict approach from the beginning. They disclosed expected loan losses and assigned realistic values to real estate and other assets. Two banks accounting for one-fifth of all Swedish banking assets were declared insolvent. The crisis cost taxpayers 4% of GDP in government support (see *What lessons can be drawn from recent financial crises? — the Swedish experience*, Riksbank speech by Urban Backstrom, August 1997).

On average, the World Bank economists found that "governments spent an average of nearly 13% of GDP cleaning up their financial systems" as a result of the accommodating bailout programmes. If they had not adopted such bailout programmes, the cost would have been 1% of GDP on average. And there was no evidence that opting for the 'accommodating' approach reduced the impact on the wider economy or avoided an economic recession — indeed, on the contrary.

Patterns of systemic banking crises (%)

Country	Crisis year	Fiscal cost (share of GDP)	Real chg in GDP	Chg in exc. rate	Decline in real asset prices
Finland	1992	11.0	-4.6	-5.5	-34.6
Indonesia	1998	50.0	-15.4	-57.5	-78.5
Rep of Korea	1998	37.0	-10.6	-28.8	-45.9
Malaysia	1998	16.4	-12.7	-13.9	-79.9
Mexico	1995	19.3	-6.2	-39.8	-53.3
Philippines	1998	0.5	-0.8	-13.0	-67.2
Sweden	1991	4.0	-3.3	1.0	-6.8
Thailand	1998	32.8	-5.4	-13.7	-77.4

Figure 15. *Source: World Bank, FDIC, Independent Strategy*

nature what it is, the banks would use the central bank's liquidity injection to postpone the day of reckoning and avoid recognition of the solvency issue.

If, in order to maintain financial system integrity, the central bank forced a bad financial institution to merge with a good one, the result could be avoidance of 'price discovery' for the bad institution's assets because they would be shielded by the strength of the good institution (this could affect the assets and liabilities of other players and delay resolution of the solvency issue on a wider scale). This is precisely what happened with Bank of America's forced merger with Merrill Lynch in the US and Lloyds' forced merger with HBoS in the UK (Figure 16).

Just lending huge dollops of liquidity without cleansing balance sheets sharply increases the eventual economic and fiscal costs of any bailout. The fiscal costs are boosted because the means of preventing private sector deleveraging is to add state leverage, creating excessive sovereign debt that then becomes the next chapter of the credit crisis.

And yet bailing out or supporting insolvent financial institutions won't avoid economic pain — indeed it can well prolong it as the Japanese example of the 1990s demonstrated and we fear may happen now.

Forced mergers

Bank of America took over the largest investment bank in the world at the time, Merrill Lynch, in the midst of the financial panic that had led to the bankruptcy of Lehman Brothers. The price was $29bn. The takeover was put together by the US Treasury and the Fed in order to ensure that contagion did not spread from the Lehman's collapse. Merrill's soaring losses were not revealed at the time nor the decision of the Merrill board to pay out $3.6bn in bonuses. Bank of America received $45bn in government funding to carry out the acquisition. It has subsequently paid this back, minus $5bn in net losses. The government also guaranteed $118bn of Bank of America assets.

In the UK, to avoid a systemic crisis, the government waived competition rules and insisted that Lloyds Bank take over HBoS, the UK's biggest mortgage lender, which had made £15bn losses in 2008-9. The UK government then took large equity stakes in the merged bank (41%) in return for government financing of £17bn. The merged bank did not return to profit until Q1'10 as dud assets remain on the books (some £24bn was written down in 2009).

Figure 16. *Source: Independent Strategy*

Ironically, much of the bible on the proper way to deal with credit crises was written by Americans, some of whom acted as consultants to the Riksbank during the Swedish crisis of the early 1990s. The same procedures were successfully applied in many Asian countries, such as Korea, to deal with their (1997) banking crisis. Partly, as a result, the downturn in their economies was relatively short-lived, leverage was rapidly reduced and their economies all emerged stronger.

The US never tired of recommending the same model to the Japanese authorities after Japan's bubble economy collapsed. Japan ignored them, took ten years to clean up its house, wasted huge fiscal resources in vain attempts to bolster demand and suffered a lost decade and a half of growth as a result.

Now the US risks the same fate by failing to apply its own medicine to itself. Instead, US monetary policy has focused on making it cheap to stay leveraged, keeping the banks holding their dud assets or buying the dud assets from the banks, so giving them free money to plough into carry trades like financing government bonds. By doing so, banks make a lot of money. This meets one government objective: healing banks' balance sheets. It is then hoped that the banks will resume lending to the consumers and corporations. That has not happened.

The authorities are also underpricing short-term capital so as to reignite a mammoth bubble in their own debt (and other asset) markets. In other words, they are making sure no-one gets paid to own cash, which means that those 'mindless of risk' are back hunting yield and ignoring risk by buying government bonds or equities.

Bankers in all major economies are doing exactly what their Japanese peers did to earn a buck and salvage themselves from insolvency in Japan's post-bubble economy. The banks are taking zero-cost money by the truckload from the Fed, the BoE, the BoJ and the ECB, putting it together with their rising deposit base, and buying government bonds further out along the curve.

Quantitative easing: success or failure?

Quantitative easing (QE) or 'unconventional measures' by central banks are where the monetary authorities seek to ease monetary policy significantly by purchasing debt (government bonds, agency bonds, asset-backed securities or corporate bonds) and equities. Central bank purchases provide the financial institutions with cash to lend onto the 'real economy' or invest in other financial assets like equities; and can be used to remove 'dud' assets from their books. No action is taken to sterilise the liquidity injected by QE.

Does QE bring about a boost to bank lending in the real economy? The evidence of 2009 would suggest not, as bank loans have contracted in the US and the UK, the countries with the biggest QE programmes.

In 2004, the Japanese authorities resorted to QE with the BoJ (Bank of Japan) making outright 'rinban' purchases of JGBs. The BoJ balance sheet rose 35% in one year and continued to rise until QE was stopped in Q2'06. The BoJ maintained existing QE beyond that date, but stopped its outright JGB purchases. According to the BoJ itself, QE helped stabilise the Japanese financial system, but it had no effect on economic recovery. Little of the increase in the quantity of money was lent on by the banking system to the real economy. It's been the same story for QE during this crisis.

Figure 17. *Source: Independent Strategy*

This investment is a zero-cost, zero-risk one that earns an infinite return on the banks' own capital (because it uses none of it!).

Who would want to dirty their hands lending to the real economy when round-tripping is so well remunerated?

Most central banks in this crisis have resorted to quantitative easing (QE) programmes, namely buying government bonds or even asset-backed securities from banks so that they can shore up their balance sheets, improve liquidity and have the cash to lend or invest (Figure 17). But have these QE schemes worked or merely added to sovereign debt liabilities?

Central banks, in using sovereign bond and other asset purchases as the means of distributing money to the banks, are funding the buying of sovereign debt that competes with their own purchases. So banks make money out of their sovereign bond investments and insure their risk.

That keeps everyone happy; the politicians get cheap money; the commercial banks make money and the central banks keep the system liquid. No wonder private investors have been participating. But this free lunch will end up being anything but!

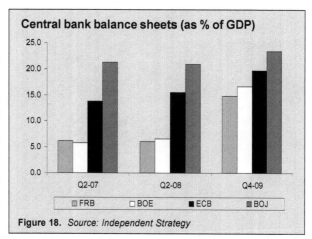

Central bank balance sheets (as % of GDP)

Figure 18. *Source: Independent Strategy*

QE has pushed the Bank of England (BoE)'s balance sheet to its highest since the end of the Second World War. The BoE's assets and liabilities now amount to around 17% of the UK's GDP. It's the same story at the Fed (Figure 18).

These policies are the antithesis of what should have been done in the aftermath of a credit bubble. Deleveraging should be allowed to wipe out the excesses of the credit cycle — excesses manifest in resource allocation (e.g. bloated financial, real estate and construction sectors), in asset prices as well as in spending and saving habits.

The aim should be to recast economic growth, founded upon thrift and productive investment. Policies should allow prices to adjust in relative terms, so that the prices of ex-bubble assets become cheap in terms of the residual wealth and earnings power of society. It is this latter process that allows for a 'natural' economic recovery based on minimum government and central bank-induced distortions.

One of our key themes has been that the collapse of New Monetarism would involve big deleveraging over many years. Indeed, according to a study by McKinsey, deleveraging does not usually start for two years after a financial crisis, followed by several years of debt decline averaging a cumulative 25% of GDP, with real GDP actually contracting for two years (Figure 19).

The causes of today's economic crisis are both *ultimate*

Deleveraging is inevitable

In a review of 45 episodes of deleveraging (reducing significantly the total debt to GDP ratio) in ten advanced economies and four emerging economies since 1930, McKinsey found that deleveraging took a long time (six to seven years) and reduced the overall debt/GDP ratio by 25% on average.

Since the crisis started, private sector (excluding the financial sector) debt has declined only slightly. Financial sector leverage has fallen considerably. But since public debt has spiralled, gross leverage for most large nations has risen.

So if deleveraging is inevitable after a financial crisis, much of it is still to come. From a historical perspective, the current challenge is not entirely unprecedented. The UK and US have slashed vast debt burdens before and McKinsey has identified four dozen smaller deleveraging episodes around the world since 1950.

But while governments have sometimes softened this task before by creating rapid growth, often by exports (via devaluation), through a peace dividend (after a war), or by reducing the real debt burden through inflation, those routes do not offer an easy escape this time. Growth, in other words, could be tough to achieve. So that leaves three, unpalatable options, McKinsey suggests, namely outright default, inflation or belt-tightening. McKinsey consequently forecasts a grim climate of austerity for the next decade.

Debt and deleveraging: the global credit bubble and the consequences, January 2010

Figure 19. *Source: McKinsey*

and *proximate*. The ultimate cause is the engrained thriftless societal behaviour of the US and many other economies over the last two decades: instant gratification of 'needs' without reference to the ability to earn the wherewithal for doing so. This did away with the economic virtue of thrift and encouraged excessive consumption.

Excessive consumption resulted in global imbalances such as the US current account deficit and other distortions (Figure 20). The mirror of excess US consumption was over-dependence on export-driven Asian 'factory' economies such as China; and excess savings in these same factory economies needed to finance the US current account deficit.

The proximate cause of the crisis is how the ultimate cause was financed: the excess credit and liquidity creation of New Monetarism. New Monetarism, or the tools of excess credit creation, is nothing but the financial circuitry that funded the leverage, asset price inflation, the dearth of savings and the consumption boom that created the crisis.

The proximate causes of the crisis cannot be addressed without the ultimate causes being so and *vice versa*. Any attempt to prolong the credit party will only prolong and worsen the ultimate causes of it. Instead of focusing on ultimate causes of the crisis, policy has concentrated on the proximate causes (the broken credit machine that financed the excesses). In place of seeking to address the real issues of lack of consumer thrift and too much borrowing, the remedial policies applied were for more credit and boosts to consumption! This will only lead to an extension of the credit crisis, but now with its locus in the public sector.

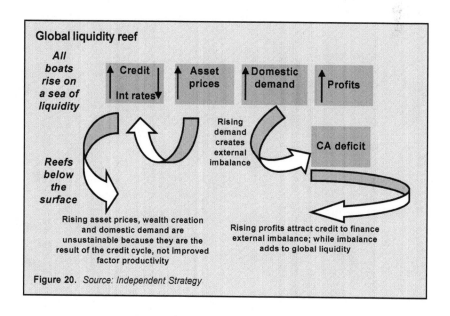

Figure 20. *Source: Independent Strategy*

CHAPTER THREE

Society in denial

"What's happening in our market today is that we have just a broad shortage of financing available. And what the government needs to do in that context... is to try to make sure that the government and the central bank together can provide the financing to help get those markets working. And that will make it more likely that these assets are worth and will have the value that is their basic inherent economic value rather than an artificially depressed value that reflects the absence of financing and credit." Timothy Geithner, US Treasury Secretary, 2008

Economics is the statistical expression of mass psychology. Mass psychology blanks out individual quirks and neuroses and focuses on society's. The process of aggregation replaces the individual with the common denominators of history and culture as the determining attributes.

Psychonomics — where mass psychology meets economic reality — is helpful in interpreting the societal, political, economic and investment worlds. For example, psychonomics can explain why the economic model that made Japan and Germany so rich, with scant reference to the free market or maximisation of shareholder wealth, would have made America poor.

Similarly, the French regularly elect and only have a choice between governments that always spend more than half of what the electorate earns. But the *vox populi* is happy with the result: among the best public transport, roads, phone services, public utilities and healthcare in the world. Yet the same model in Italy simply makes tax fraud the country's largest industry and produces a state of quasi-permanent fiscal insolvency from which Italy is saved daily by membership of the Eurozone.

In a nutshell: psychonomics preaches the truth of there being no ultimate economic truth, theory or model. There are simply things that work because they suit the mindset of the people who live in the economy where they are applied. And then there are things that don't work.

Unfortunately, our current economic crisis is less about psychonomics than psychotics! The policies adopted by the authorities in the US, the UK and Japan to deal with the credit crisis and its aftermath are the result of being in denial.

It is not that our leaders were unworthy or stupid; they were and are simply ignoring reality. Psychonomics tells us that insanity is more common among the intelligent, wealthy, successful 'smart people' than the peasantry! Our leaders are simply unable to face the realities of the credit crisis. In the US, they cannot admit that the 'American dream' must be earned, not borrowed. In Japan, the politicians want to apply the same policies that have failed for the last 15 years.

The reason is that the politicians reckon that to adopt effective policies that deal with leverage and insolvency would entail such a reduction in living standards that it would be political suicide. Odd then that Mrs Thatcher got elected and re-elected in the UK back in the 1980s on just such a ticket of prudence and solvency and addressing the ultimate causes of Britain's economic woes. But the days when politicians stood for their own principles, rather than for policies that spin doctors and ad-men create to suit the masses' idea of instant gratification, are long gone. The policies now being applied as a salve to our economic wounds are warped. Warped policies result in warped economies.

Lest we forget, governments have few resources. Unless they liquidate their own assets, resources they use to 'solve' the credit crisis have to be taken from another economic player, normally one that adds more economic value. Therefore, in order to spend to solve the crisis, government can only tax or borrow.

During the Great Recession, the US government has borrowed more and taxed less. The net outcome has been and will be to transfer resources away from more productive users and invest them in low-productivity consumer support, financial bailouts and housing. This entails an economic cost. And it is far from clear that this cost will be outweighed by the benefits of future economic growth.

The problem is that, when government borrows in order to buy assets from the financial sector, these are likely to be, by definition, dud assets or financial sector players would be trading them between themselves. The government steps in to buy, say, mortgage-backed securities from the private sector using borrowed money to do so (Figure 21).

This is not a *substitute* of government debt for private sector debt. It is the *addition* of a layer of government debt to a still extant layer of private sector debt. Both debts will not cancel out until both are redeemed at maturity. Purchasing a bank loan with money raised by a US treasury bond, or using the treasury bond itself to do so, doubles the amount of debt outstanding for the underlying asset during the life of both debt securities.

At maturity, both securities (the treasury bond and the purchased loan) are liquidated. The treasury bond will always pay back 100% of its par value unless the US government defaults. But the stock of private sector debt will have experienced defaults (remember the government only gets to

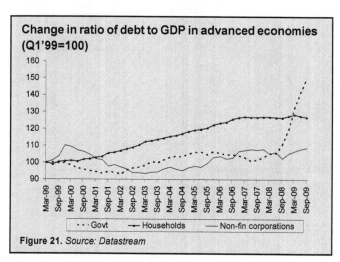

Figure 21. *Source: Datastream*

buy inferior assets). The taxpayer will have to cover these losses (adjusted for income earned by the purchased asset), in addition to the extra cost of servicing the government debt.

So it is a myth that government borrowings to purchase private sector debt can substitute good (triple A sovereign) debt for bad private sector debt. It adds a layer of public debt to private debt for the life of the purchased bond or loan. In the case of a fiscal stimulus programme funded by debt, a single layer of government debt equal to the deficit spending is added. And, as the proceeds are predominantly used to subsidise households, the result is to encourage households to stay over-indebted.

Public borrowing transfers resources from the productive sector to sectors that are quite likely to be less productive. And, by adding a layer of debt, government borrowing adds to an already highly-layered leverage system, where leveraged investors are invested in leveraged intermediaries that invest in assets of leveraged entities. Clearly, this adds to the problems of unwinding the global Ponzi scheme of excessive credit.

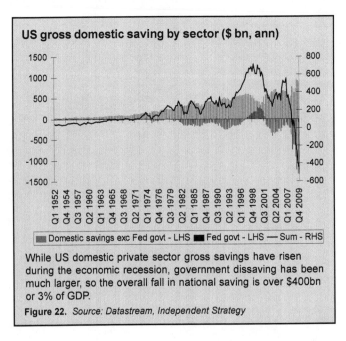

US gross domestic saving by sector ($ bn, ann)

Domestic savings exc Fed govt - LHS ■ Fed govt - LHS — Sum - RHS

While US domestic private sector gross savings have risen during the economic recession, government dissaving has been much larger, so the overall fall in national saving is over $400bn or 3% of GDP.

Figure 22. *Source: Datastream, Independent Strategy*

The US has very low private sector savings rates to meet its increased public sector deficit (Figure 22). As the consumer weakened, household savings rose. But government and public sector dissaving has rocketed as a result of deficit spending. So the increase in private sector savings has been more than offset by falls in the thrift of government. As national savings are the sum of the private and public sector savings rates, the US is suffering a *falling national saving rate*. This means that an increase in foreign funding will be needed to fund these spending programmes once the Fed stops monetising government debt through the banking system.

The US needs to achieve a reasonable and sustainable payments balance with the rest of the world. That would require a current account deficit under 3% of GDP rather than 6% seen during the credit bubble. The US public sector dissaving rate is now around 8% of GDP and will stay there for many years. That means, to achieve a reasonable external balance, the heavy lifting of the national savings rate must be done by households turning thrifty. It implies a rise in household savings rates to at least 10% of disposable income from today's 4% level. That would require a signifi-cant fall in personal consumption from here, unless household income was booming at the time. Businesses will continue to hoard cash and resist new investment as they have plenty of spare capacity. That will help increase the net national savings rate (i.e. savings net of investment). But neither source of private savings will be sufficient to overcome govern-ment dissaving.

In this significant way, the US and the UK are repeating the errors of Japan: increasing government leverage so that total leverage fails to con-tract. In Japan, this helped to condemn the country to a 'lost decade' of deflation and stagnation in the 1990s.

Japan was better off in one key respect; it had a massive stock and flow of domestic savings to finance its profligacy. Japan's emulators in the US and UK have no such support. Their household savings rates are very low. This makes their massive increases in sovereign debt financeable only by foreign savers — if the latter are foolish enough to do so. Foolish because this is about the least productive form of investment they could choose in now the world's most overpriced financial asset!

Moreover, government action to bail out the financial sector is neither temporary nor economically neutral. The new bureaucracies created to administer the expanded role of the state will remain a heavy and unproductive hand on the economic tiller well beyond the duration of the crisis itself. Their impact on efficient allocation of increasingly scarce capital is likely to be particularly deleterious. In addition, the efficient allocation of capital will be hindered by the fact that bank balance sheets will remain uncleansed of dud assets and that malinvestment from the bubble period will not have been cleared by market mechanisms.

Markets are only slowly copping on. While OECD government borrowing is set to soak up around 25% of world savings flow this year (and 50% of the OECD's), real interest rates remain close to their lows (Figure 23). Market awareness is lagging because central banks have been printing the money for financial institutions to buy sovereign debt, and buying it themselves. And households have been ploughing much of their increased precautionary savings into government bonds for safety and yield.

Received wisdom is that this 'virtuous circle' won't come undone before vigorous economic recovery returns. By then, higher yields will matter less because there will be optimism, economic growth and wealth creation. This is wrong. Excess leverage becomes a credit crisis when it does; not when it rationally should. The level of excess debt is all that matters.

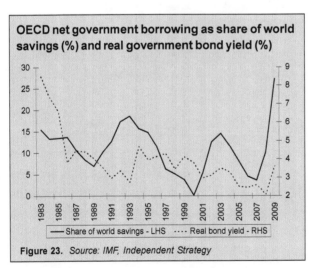

OECD net government borrowing as share of world savings (%) and real government bond yield (%)

Share of world savings - LHS ···· Real bond yield - RHS

Figure 23. Source: IMF, Independent Strategy

When we write we have to be rational (most of the time). Our theory of the next round of the credit crisis is that it will happen when the first derivative of monetary and fiscal stimulus drops to zero — in 2010 or 2011. And it will automatically do so unless the largesse of 2009 is repeated. Then the effect will be felt on financial assets and the economy.

The arithmetic works like this. If an economy grew by 1% last year because of the fiscal and monetary stimulus; in order to grow by 1% this year it would require twice last year's stimulus. First, last year's stimulus must be repeated to offset the shrinkage that would occur without it. Second, another equal (or greater) amount of stimulus is needed to make the economy expand at the same rate as last year on top of last year's achieved level. From the current position, this is unfinanceable.

The Keynesians will retort that the initial fiscal stimulus will have set in motion a bunch of multipliers that will make each $1 of state spending grow by much more than a $1. And the Keynesian monetarists (yup, they exist too!) will claim that the same applies to monetary stimulus.

The Keynesians will also say that it doesn't matter how the state spends: if aggregate demand is slack, the spending plugs a deflationary gap. But that ignores balance sheets and behaviour. Using savings to spend on things that reduce the value of those savings down the road is simply accumulating piecemeal insolvency. Insolvency will become a credit crisis when the liquidity to fund it dries up. Peoples' reaction to the deterioration in the solvency of future saving will be to make them save more and spend less.

The quality of fiscal spending is the key issue in determining the solvency of state leverage. Theorists ignore this. But it matters. A national economy that is divided by a large river which has no bridge will benefit from a bridge built by government. This is a productive investment. A thriftless nation of insolvent borrowers will benefit little from government subsidies to keep them in their overleveraged and unaffordable homes. This is unproductive spending.

The impact of fiscal multipliers

The IMF recently did a study on the impact of fiscal multipiers in different countries[1]. The fiscal multiplier is the ratio of the change in output to an exogenous change in the fiscal deficit. The size of the multiplier should be larger if 'leakages' are few. Leakages are minimised and the impact of fiscal spending on growth is maximised if: a stimulus package has a higher government spending component relative to tax cuts; the marginal propensity to consume is large; measures are targeted to liquidity-constrained consumers; there is little impact of the 'Ricardian effect' on curbing spending because of future tax increases; the propensity to import is small; automatic stabilisers are small; and the size of the 'output gap' is small.

Economists disagree on the impact of fiscal multipliers with estimates for the US varying between 0.5-1.5 on nominal growth for every dollar of fiscal stimulus. Robert Barro reckons that the peacetime fiscal multiplier for the US is close to zero (see *Government spending is no free lunch*, WSJ, 22 January 2009)! The IMF estimated that advanced economies could expect a fiscal multiplier of no more than 0.4-0.6 (see *Fiscal multipliers*, May 2009, IMF staff paper). The Centre for Economic Policy Research (CEPR) recently presented new research using quarterly data for 45 countries from 1960 to 2007 (see *How big are fiscal multipliers?*, CEPR Policy Insight No 39, October 2009). They found that advanced economies could expect no more than a multiplier of 0.24 when comparing a 1% rise in government consumption to GDP growth. For developing countries, the initial impact was close to zero. However, over a period of up to six years, the cumulative effect was 1.04 for advanced countries and 0.79 for developing countries. The 0.79 multiplier implies that each additional dollar of government consumption in developing economies crowds out some other component of GDP by 21 cents over the long run.

Figure 24. *Source: Independent Strategy*

We see little evidence that these famed Keynesian spending multipliers are working to boost consumption or investment (Figure 24). And as for credit multipliers, the banks would have to lend for that to happen and the banks aren't lending. "Ah but" the Keynesians will say: "it's just a matter of time. It's all about lags". We think it is about reality, not lags.

1. *A Mody, F Ohnsorge*, After the crisis, *IMF working paper 1011*, January 2010

CHAPTER FOUR

The sovereign debt explosion

Sovereign debt levels have exploded. And these higher levels are set to become self-perpetuating.

In 2010, the OECD area-wide fiscal deficit is projected to peak at a post-war high of around 8.25% of GDP. Public debt will average more than 100% of GDP in the Group of 20 advanced economies by 2014, up 40 percentage points from 2007[1] (Figure 25).

Gross public sector borrowing needs for the OECD area increased from $9trn in 2007 to around $16trn in 2009, with much the same level of borrowing in 2010. Net borrowing (after redemptions) has increased from around $500bn in 2007 to a staggering $3.5trn in 2009[2]. That is equivalent to two-thirds of all annual productive investment in the OECD.

Over the past three years, public debt has grown rapidly in countries where it had remained relatively low before the crisis. Although the rise in debt levels is comparatively small in countries with a history of debt problems (such as Italy and Greece), the crisis has, nevertheless, added fuel to their problems.

Financial rescue programmes, including capital injection, Treasury purchases of assets and lending (but not debt guarantees), amount to 13.2% of GDP in advanced economies so far, pretty much the average for previous finan-

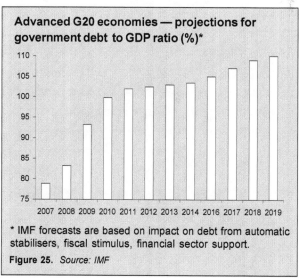

Advanced G20 economies — projections for government debt to GDP ratio (%)*

* IMF forecasts are based on impact on debt from automatic stabilisers, fiscal stimulus, financial sector support.

Figure 25. *Source: IMF*

cial crises. But overall fiscal balances (net of government financial rescue programmes) has risen by 20-30% pts of GDP in just three years. Even more worrying is that most of the projected deficits are structural rather than cyclical in nature. The structural contribution to the rise in the deficits ranges from over 70% in the UK, the US and Japan, over 60% in Germany and France to only 10% in Italy. So many of these deficits will persist, even during the cyclical recovery.

Reinhart and Rogoff found that three years after a typical banking crisis the absolute level of public debt is on average about 86% larger than prior to the crisis[3]. In those countries where the crisis was most severe, debt almost trebled. This time around, several countries are beyond this historical average: Ireland with increases in public debt of 98% between 2007 and 2009 and the United Kingdom with projected rises of 111% by 2011. The US and Spain (with projected increases of 75% and 78%, respectively, by 2011) are not far behind.

At such high levels of debt, the differential between the interest rate and output growth is the critical parameter in determining the future evolution of public debt. When this differential is negative, so that the interest rate is below the growth rate, the debt ratio is generally bounded. By contrast, when it is positive, the debt ratio tends to increase exponentially.

The key relationship is then between the level of public debt and two major indicators of the budgetary stance — the primary balance (excluding interest payments on the outstanding debt) and the structural primary balance (the primary balance adjusted for cyclical increases in expenditure and decreases in revenue). The higher the positive differential between the real interest-rate and potential output growth, the larger the required structural primary surplus will have to be to maintain a stable debt-to-GDP ratio* (Figure 26).

* The primary budget surplus needed to stabilise the debt to GDP ratio = debt/GDP x interest-rate on debt less GDP growth rate. Both rates must be either nominal or real. In an economy with 100% of debt to GDP, a primary budget balance will keep the debt ratio constant. However, if the interest rate on the debt exceeds GDP growth by, say 3% pts, a primary surplus of 3% of GDP would be needed to stabilise the debt ratio.

The dynamics of debt

The dynamics of public debt depend on three factors: the level of real interest payments; the primary budget balance (the balance of government spending less interest payments on debt and government revenues); and changes in the nominal value of the stock of government liabilities, often called seignorage.

If the real interest rate on debt is higher than real output growth, the debt to GDP ratio will increase even if a government manages to maintain its primary budget in balance. For the debt to GDP ratio to stay constant, the difference between the real interest rate and real GDP growth must be matched by a primary budget surplus. If new debt is added, interest payments will increase, thus leading to ever greater amounts of debt, unless a primary budget surplus is run. This spiral of debt from rising interest rates is in effect a 'Ponzi' scheme, where more borrowing is raised to service what has been already borrowed.

What is a country's sustainable debt level? That will depend on the fiscal capacity of a country (how far tax revenues can be raised without causing the tax base to shrink or how far public spending can be cut without social disruption). It will also depend on the response of bond markets to government policy and the state of public finances. One good way of measuring the sustainability of public debt levels is to measure the magnitude of the primary budget surplus required over time for its debt ratio to be stabilised at some suitable level.

If real GDP growth rises faster than the real interest rate, then the debt-to-GDP ratio will fall as long as the primary budget is in balance. But if the primary budget is in deficit, faster growth may not be sufficient to get the debt ratio down. A big problem for many governments is that the primary budget deficit is structural and is not reduced by faster economic growth because government spending is in 'mandatory' areas like health, education or pensions. Over three-quarters of the primary deficit is structural in many OECD countries.

Overall fiscal balances, 2010 (% of GDP)

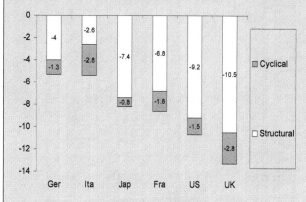

Figure 26. *Source: BIS, Independent Strategy*

So far, the build-up of public debt in industrial countries has taken place against the backdrop of an exceedingly low interest-rate environment. Despite low inflation, the real interest rate (in effective terms) at which governments are able to finance their deficits and roll over outstanding debt obligations has been falling since the late 1990s, reaching almost zero in some countries in the wake of the monetary policy response to the financial crisis.

However, the situation is changing quickly even without a change in monetary policy-controlled interest rates. Real borrowing rates rose through 2009 and are poised to continue increasing with the reversal of the current zero interest-rate policies of many OECD authorities.

Today more than 40% of global GDP is accounted for by countries (overwhelmingly in the advanced economies) running fiscal deficits of 10% of GDP or more! For much of the past 30 years, only 5% of GDP was in countries with such deficits and mainly in emerging economies[4].

Unless the stance of fiscal policy changes, by 2020 the primary deficit-to-GDP ratio will rise to 13% in Ireland; 8–10% in Japan, Spain, the United Kingdom and the United States; and 3–7% in Austria, Belgium, Germany, Greece, the Netherlands and Portugal. Only in Italy do these policy settings keep the primary deficits relatively well contained — a consequence of the fact that the country entered the crisis with a nearly balanced budget and did not implement any real stimulus over the past several years.

But the biggest impact will be on the size of sovereign debt. Without any action, debt-to-GDP ratios will rise rapidly in the next decade, exceeding 300% of GDP in Japan; 200% in the UK; and 150% in Belgium, France, Ireland, Greece, Italy and the US. And it will get progressively worse as the share of debt absorbed by interest payments alone rises from 5% today to over 10% in all cases, and as high as 30% in the UK!

What level of primary balance would be required to bring the debt-to-GDP ratio in each country back to its pre-crisis, 2007 level? To achieve that within five years from now would mean generating an average annual primary surplus of 8–10% of GDP in the US, Japan, the UK and Ireland and 5–7% in a number of other countries. In 2009, the US government ran a primary budget deficit of 10% of GDP, while the UK and Japan had primary deficits around 6% of GDP. So the fiscal tightening required is staggering, if not impossible (Figure 27). Even if a less-demanding time schedule was applied, say over ten years to achieve 2007 sovereign debt/GDP levels, the fiscal tightening (the swing) required would be 15% of GDP in the US and 12% in the UK and Japan!

The impact of the rising cost of sovereign debt on budget arithmetic will also be rapid because the duration of government debt is generally short (except for the UK). Even in the US, the duration of the stock of government debt is low at only 55 months (Figure 28). Moreover, according to the OECD, governments will be issuing mostly short-term paper in 2010, as they did in 2009 — around 62% of total issuance.

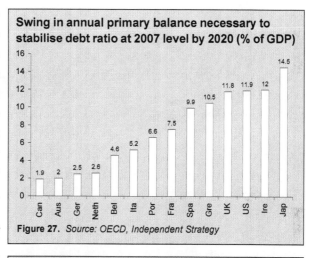

Figure 27. *Source: OECD, Independent Strategy*

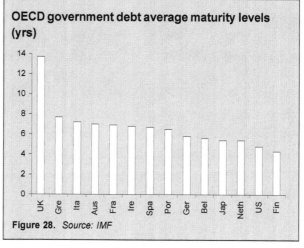

Figure 28. *Source: IMF*

THE SOVEREIGN DEBT EXPLOSION

This means that, as sovereign yields rise, they quickly translate into increased cost of debt because the stock of old debt is replaced rapidly with new, more expensive, debt. So governments cannot inoculate themselves from the effect of rising yields.

Within five years, interest payments on the stock of government debt would triple if inflation settled at 5-6%. In Japan, if government bonds got to the same yield as those in Germany, it would cost the Japanese budget 12% (instead of today's 3%) of total spending and nearly double the current 12% of GDP deficit!

A sovereign debt crisis will not unfold like a private sector one because governments can theoretically avoid default on their debt by printing money and debasing their currency with inflation. Governments can also up taxation and reduce spending in ways that aren't available to an over-leveraged private sector in crisis — and their customers are often captive taxpayers who cannot flee. Governments, in an act of economic repression, can also force its bonds on unwilling buyers, like captive financial institutions. And markets always assume a lower default risk for sovereigns than for private sector creditors. This may slow the spread of the sovereign global credit crisis.

One way to bring down sovereign debt to GDP ratios is to make GDP grow by a bigger percentage than the cost of the debt. It doesn't matter if the GDP growth is real or nominal — the difference being inflation — provided nominal growth is larger than nominal interest rates.

In the US, rapid nominal growth brought public sector debt down from 109% of GDP in 1946 to just 36% of GDP in 2003. But the US post-war experience was anomalous. A rapid decline in defence spending yielded a significant 'peace dividend' in terms of real GDP growth and helped reduce government spending. Even with the GI Bill and the Korean War, defence spending tumbled from 37% of GDP in 1945 to 11% by 1955, bringing the deficit from 12% of GDP in 1945 to outright surplus by 1947.

The financial markets also tolerated higher inflation during this period in a way that they would not do today. This increased nominal GDP at a time when the stock of debt was declining anyway, which resulted in a faster reduction in the ratio of sovereign debt to GDP. In a study of the decline in the US sovereign debt to GDP ratio between 1946 and 2003, Morgan Stanley found that the annual reduction of 2.9% points was achieved by real growth for 1.3% pts and by 1.6% pts through inflation[5].

Official estimates of gross public debt today are seriously underestimating the real level of public sector leverage. Take the UK's public debt. It excludes government-guaranteed bank debt because it expects UK banks to replace this debt with normal debt as the guaranteed debt matures. Over £300bn of the maturing debt that the banks had to raise to replace destroyed assets during the financial crisis was backed by the UK government in the form of £134bn of state guarantees and £178bn of treasury bills provided by the Bank of England in exchange for the banks' dud mortgage-backed securities.

This debt will mature by 2012 and there is no way that the banks can fund these redemptions from increased deposits. The funding gap is just too great. If the government agrees to roll over this debt and extend the guarantees, then that debt will look like a long-term liability of the state and should become part of the public sector debt (adding another 20% of GDP to a ratio that will already be pushing 90%!). The UK is not alone in having a banking sector facing a major funding problem (Figure 29) — globally,

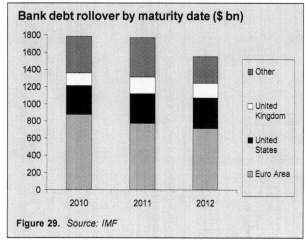

Figure 29. *Source: IMF*

nearly $5trn of bank debt is due to mature in the next three years, just as government issuance surges.

It's the same sort of story in the US. US banks have a funding gap (between assets in the form of loans and mortgages and customer deposits) equal to more than one-third of their assets. This used to be funded by wholesale money markets. Now the Fed and the US Treasury plug the gap. The same arithmetic as for the UK applies: either the banks are thrown back on funding themselves with a vastly increased issuance of bonds that will compete with US treasuries or the gap will continue to be funded by the authorities, adding to the stock of sovereign bonds.

The US government also provides guarantees for the lending and debt issuance of the so-called Government Sponsored Enterprises (GSEs) in home mortgages, Fannie Mae and Freddie Mac. They were taken into 'conservatorship' when they went bust in 2009. The GSEs have provided over 70% of new mortgage originations in 2009 and are basically holding up the residential housing market. But they continue to lose money and leak asset value. They will have to be supported by the taxpayer for the foreseeable future. And yet none of these GSE liabilities or their assets are currently included in US public sector debt calculations. That would add over $5trn to the gross debt, or another 35% of GDP!

As frightening as it is to consider public debt in OECD economies increasing to more than 100% of GDP, an even greater danger arises from a rapidly ageing population. The related unfunded liabilities are large and growing and should be a central part of today's long-term fiscal planning. The ratio of old-age population to working-age population is projected to rise sharply in OECD countries. This rise is particularly acute in countries such as Japan, Spain, Italy and Greece, which are already laden with relatively high debts.

In the US, the Congressional Budget Office (CBO) says that the social security fund is now taking in less in contributions than it is spending on benefits for the first time ever! In order to meet its age-related spending liabilities, the CBO reckons the US would need a permanent improvement in its annual budget balance of the order of 2.6% of 2009 GDP in the next 50 years and 3.2% in 75 years.

Added to population ageing is the problem posed by rising health care costs. US health care expenditures as a percentage of GDP are expected to double from about 5% today to 10% by 2035 and more than treble to 17% by 2080.

Any attempt by governments to inflate away their debts will face several hurdles. First, market participants seem unlikely to be fooled by unexpected inflation — certainly not for sufficiently long or by enough to dent the debt. Despite what some might view as inflation complacency, the transformation of financial markets over the past 50 years, including the growing use of instruments to protect against inflation, suggests much more sensitivity to inflation risks than in the post-war period.

Second, in the US nearly half of federal government outlays are linked to inflation, meaning that increments to debt would rise with inflation. Social security, which accounts for one-quarter of all outlays, is officially indexed and Medicare and Medicaid are 'unofficially' indexed. Indeed, over the period 2009-20, the US CBO estimates that these three programmes will account for 72% of the growth in total federal outlays and about the same share of the growth in debt.

Even setting aside all those hurdles, with core inflation declining again, it would take some time to boost inflation sufficiently to erode the debt. That's all the more reason to pay attention to the other ways that fiscal pressures may vent in financial markets.

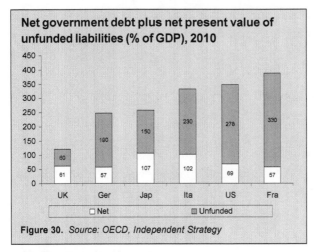

Net government debt plus net present value of unfunded liabilities (% of GDP), 2010

Figure 30. *Source: OECD, Independent Strategy*

First among these are unfunded state pension liabilities (future benefits not covered by future contributions). These far outweigh the high levels of official sovereign debt (Figure 30). According to research by Jag Gokhale, an economist at the Cato Institute in Washington[7], bringing future pension obligations onto government balance sheets would raise government debt levels in France to 549% of GDP and 418% in Germany. Of course, these numbers are arguable, depending on the discount rates used. The OECD estimates of unfunded sovereign liabilities are lower, but worrying nevertheless. Outstanding unfunded liabilities are huge and would be difficult to meet even without the present crisis (Figure 31).

For all these reasons, the impact of the sovereign debt explosion on the major economies of the world will be different this time from what happened to Japan in the 1990s or in the previous debt crises that Reinhart and Rogoff have measured. That's because the governments of these economies will all have to feed from the same trough of international savings.

Put simply, sovereign credit risk may not immediately create inflation risk; it may instead translate into real interest-rate or currency risk. Indeed, our forecast for a rise in nominal ten-year treasury yields to 5.5% is a story about real rates, in which a revival of private credit demands collides with massive treasury borrowing needs.

Global investors will likely demand a price (higher yields) to buy US debt, or they will diversify away from it. Financial markets will, when provoked, find ways to 'punish the printers' — in this case, meaning those governments with fiscal policies that are clearly on an unsustainable path and which are likely to press central banks to print money to finance them.

The rise in the cost of sovereign debt will also seriously damage the value of global banking assets, as the value of the claims on government (namely holdings of government bonds) would fall. For example, Japanese banks have 22% of their assets in government bonds, Italian banks 12%, Canadian banks 9% and even US banks hold 6% in government securities. Moreover, the cost of financing for banks would rise as sovereign bond yields rose. Bank debt could not be seen as less risky than sovereign debt and so the cost of raising it would increase. This would increase the cost of capital to the real economy, so depressing growth.

Sovereign debt risk and unfunded state liabilities

The measure of gross sovereign debt excludes the unfunded liabilities of the state, mostly future age-related healthcare and pension rights. Adding these to the gross sovereign debt figures makes the picture far darker. Unfunded liabilities are becoming increasingly relevant because in our ageing societies they are turning into costs today and providing an increasingly tough headwind for any government trying to tighten fiscal policy or reduce its debts.

Including unfunded liabilities in sovereign debt changes the pecking order of the states most at risk from a credit crisis. For example, because Japan has relatively low unfunded liabilities, it comes out better than the US on a measure of total sovereign liabilities (including the unfunded ones) to GDP.

However, we accord unfunded liabilities less weight than the gross sovereign debt figures for two reasons. First, unfunded liabilities turn into a liquid drain on the states coffers relatively slowly and can be modified over time. It's like cooking a frog slowly in water that gradually heats up to boiling point. The frog never jumps out and eventually dies. It takes a liquidity crisis, the equivalent of plunging the frog into already boiling water, to make the poor beast react and try to save itself.

Second, unfunded liabilities are by definition almost 100% domesticated and owed by the state to its own citizens. As we discuss in the next chapter, domesticated debt is much less likely to turn into a liquidity crisis that sparks a sovereign debt crisis than when foreigners fund a high share of sovereign debt.

Figure 31. *Source: Independent Strategy*

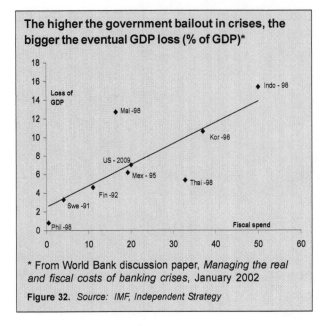

The higher the government bailout in crises, the bigger the eventual GDP loss (% of GDP)*

* From World Bank discussion paper, *Managing the real and fiscal costs of banking crises*, January 2002

Figure 32. *Source: IMF, Independent Strategy*

Post-crisis economic growth will provide little help in reducing the sovereign debt/GDP ratio (Figure 32). It will be hampered by the use of policies that prolong excesses in order to fight the credit crisis and thus damage future productivity (Figure 33). As the crisis is widespread and its errors and excesses broadly shared, there will no dynamic area of the global economy for the afflicted economies to lean on while they deleverage.

1. *The state of public finances: outlook after 2008 crisis*, IMF, March 2009

2. *The surge in borrowing needs of OECD governments, revised estimates*, OECD financial market trends, December 2009

3. Reinhart and Rogoff op cit.

4. Willem Buiter, Citibank, March 2010

5. Morgan Stanley

6. DTZ, March 2010

7. *Measuring the unfunded obligations of European countries*, Jagadeesh Gokhale, National Center for Policy Analysis, January 2009

8. EU Commission Quarterly Report, T*he impact of the economic and financial crisis on potential growth*, Cabanillas, McMorrow, Mourre

Pattern of growth in aggregate supply after crisis

Chart A: Scenario 1 — loss in potential output level entirely recouped over time

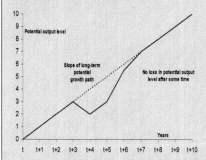

Chart B: Scenario 2 — no change in long-run potential growth — permanent loss in output level

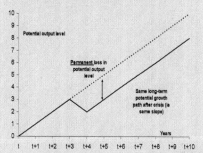

Chart C: Scenario 3 — permanent loss in output level and potential growth

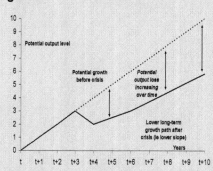

What shape will the economy take on over the next decade? There are two variables to be considered: productivity and the output loss caused by the credit crisis. There are three options. These show trend or potential output before the crisis extrapolated into the future (dotted line) and actual output (full line). Chart A projects a rapid V-shaped recovery for lost output and a return to the same potential growth path as before the crisis.

Chart B forecasts productivity and potential growth being the same before and after the crisis, which means the output lost during the crisis is not regained. Chart C shows what happens if productivity has been durably damaged and reduces potential growth permanently after the crisis. In this case, the output loss is not recouped and, because of reduced productivity, the gap grows between the trend output before and after the crisis. The markets are anticipating a rapid return to business as usual as in Chart A. We reckon Chart C (permanent loss of output, productivity and growth) is the most likely.

Figure 33. *Source: EU Commission*[8]

CHAPTER FIVE

The Keynesian identity

The consensus view of the post-credit crisis landscape is that prolonged fiscal and monetary stimulus is necessary to ensure sustainable OECD economic growth. The protagonists of prolonged fiscal stimulus (Bernanke, Krugman, Stiglitz etc) make the argument that the economy is a twin-piston engine. Rising government dissaving is the result of falling private demand and thus of rising private saving.

This is neat Keynesian economics. If the private piston of growth goes down, the public sector piston of growth must go up. The marginal savings surplus in the private sector must be matched by the marginal decrease in savings by the public sector. If not, the economy will lapse into depression or recession due to an excess of savings and a dearth of demand.

But this analysis is flawed. It considers the economy only in terms of flows and ignores balance sheet effects. This is much like looking at a corporation's income statement and ignoring its balance sheet and the fund flow statements that connect both. Keynesian identities will always balance by definition. But they can result from a variety of different consumption/savings/investment choices that are themselves affected by stock (balance sheet) considerations.

Take the example where a move to smaller government reduced public sector dissaving (its deficit) and its stock of debt. The response would very probably be a boost to GDP growth from smaller bureaucracy, an increase in private sector wealth (falling risk-free interest rates) and from more productive use of resources (including capital). Some of that increase in private sector wealth could be spent without reducing private sector savings from income (though the national accounting conventions might show it as a savings reduction — quite incorrectly).

In this case, on a flow basis, the government savings rate would have risen while the private sector savings rate (from income) would be the same and the economy would be booming. The positive impacts are clearly the result of smaller government: reduced public sector dissavings and rising wealth. The savings balances calculated on a flow basis would have foreseen lower growth due to rising aggregate savings (government saves more and households on an income-flow basis save the same). But the effects could be intensified by balance sheet impacts. The opposite also applies: rising government dissaving ultimately destroys debt value and, instead of boosting future growth, diminishes it.

The savings balance approach to economic growth is also confusing in another respect. It says that the sum of public sector savings, private sector savings and the current account (with its sign reversed) must sum to zero. A current account deficit equates to the amount of savings that foreigners must provide over the capital account to offset the dearth of domestic national savings. A current account surplus means the country has to export capital equal to its domestic savings surplus. This is true by definition. But again the argument is incomplete.

If a government increases its savings rate while the private sector keeps its own savings rate constant, the economy will shrink unless the current account improves (through increased net exports) reducing the need for foreign savings. But the savings definition used in this argument is actu-ally *net* savings — the surplus of gross savings over gross investment for both government and the private sector.

Gross domestic savings can rise, but the economy can still have the same external deficit if gross domestic investment rises too. For example, in the decade after the Asian crisis in 1998, Asia built up a net savings sur-plus (in Ben Bernanke's opinion 'excess saving'). But the rise in net savings was not due to rising gross savings, but falling investment (except for China in the later years).

So gross domestic savings can rise and the external deficit could stay the same or even increase if gross domestic investment also rises. And that is what would usually happen in a growing economy. The Keynesian identity is just that. On its own, it cannot provide a policy prescription for an economy (Figure 34).

The Keynesian identity: policy and prejudice

Let's look at an economy from a Keynesian view, namely in terms of expenditure. The Keynesian identity is that the Private Sector (S-I) + Public Sector (S-I) - CA = zero, where S = Savings and I = investment and CA is the current account balance. If a country like the US has both a low level of private sector savings and bigger government dissaving, it can only run a current account deficit (which will equal its drawdown of foreign savings to plug the gap). No amount of anti-Chinese protectionist rhetoric will change the reality; if the US wants to balance its current account it must save more and import less, consume less and export more and stop bashing others for sating its excessive consumer demand and profligate fiscal policies.

An argument has been presented that Germany is destroying Europe by saving and exporting too much, forcing all those poor Greeks unwillingly to consume more than they earn. Therefore the Germans should pay themselves much more to do much less and spend a goodly slice of their previously productive lives on Greek beaches being served ouzo by the newly employed Greeks. The absurdity of this may escape some economists but not common sense.

Let us assume for a moment a different chain of causality in the Keynesian identity. After all, the German share of global trade in manufactures has been stable or rising for two decades while the US and Japan's fell victim to China. So the Germans must be doing something right! Instead of being the destructive result of Germany's wicked surplus savers, let us assume that Germany's current account is positive because foreigners always want to buy more German goods than Germans want to buy foreigners' goods. Let us also assume this is because German goods are superior. Then German domestic savings will always be in surplus. Any attempt to reduce that surplus will fail unless foreigners buy less superior German goods or Germans buy more inferior foreign goods or migrate to southern beaches and Irish bogs for more prolonged vacations in increasing droves.

The proposal that Germany should boost its wage costs in order to allow the weaker European economies to export more to them is a recommendation to substitute economic mediocrity for excellence. Since when does that produce durably good results in welfare economics?

But maybe Germany should consume more of its own excellent products and deny them to foreigners. This is nonsense as the Germans have been making excellent products for such a long time that they own as much of them as they need. Of course, the Keynesians could introduce compulsory consumption of three new BMWs per year instead of two. But let's stop there!

Figure 34. *Source: Independent Strategy*

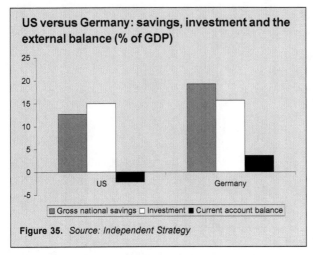

US versus Germany: savings, investment and the external balance (% of GDP)

Figure 35. *Source: Independent Strategy*

Take the contrast between Germany, which runs a current account surplus and the US, which runs a deficit (Figure 35). Both could have the same gross national savings rate. Germany actually has a gross savings ratio of 20% of GDP compared to just 11% in the US. Does that mean Germany runs a massive external surplus? — well, not quite. Given that its investment rate is 17%, it runs a current account surplus of about 3% of GDP. As the US has an investment rate of 15% (very close to Germany's), it runs a current account deficit of 4% of GDP. In the case of Germany, it invests less than it saves domestically and so has an export surplus; in the case of the US, it invests more domestically than it saves and so runs a current account deficit.

It does not follow that a rise in government dissaving is the counterpart of falling private demand and rising savings. In this crisis, US government dissaving has been far bigger than rising savings in the private sector. But the current account deficit has not widened because private investment has slumped.

There is another reason why in this crisis government dissaving exceeds by far the rise in private sector savings. Government dissaving has been monetised by central banks buying government debt or giving banks the motivation and wherewithal to do so. When public sector dissaving is monetised, its growth is not the counterpart of a rise in private sector savings.

The justification for massive fiscal spending and budget deficits in this crisis is that, given the imminent threat of a great depression, governments couldn't do anything else. This again is symptomatic of policy based on denial. There was never any risk of a Great Depression (commonly known as a debt deflation spiral) because widely dispersed price deflation never happened

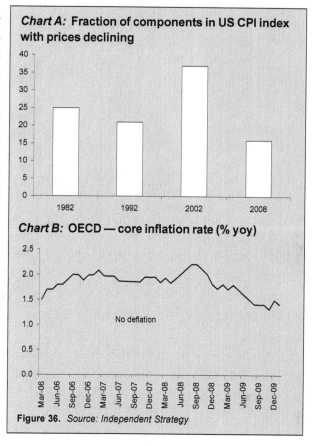

Chart A: Fraction of components in US CPI index with prices declining

Chart B: OECD — core inflation rate (% yoy)

No deflation

Figure 36. *Source: Independent Strategy*

(Figure 36). Core inflation remained positive and trade protectionism has been avoided on a major scale (so far). Indeed, the decline in asset prices, wealth or private sector spending in this recession has only cancelled a few years of excess gains.

As we explained in Chapter 2, Figure 15, when analysing 30 years of systemic banking crises across 94 countries, the World Bank[1] asked the question "did countries that used accommodating policies experience faster economic recovery?" The answer was: "We failed to uncover evidence that this was the case. Indeed, such support seems to have prolonged crises because recovery took longer".

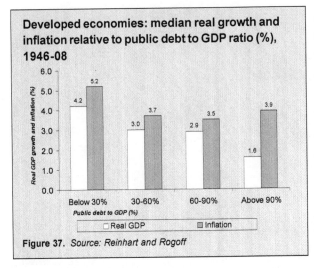

Developed economies: median real growth and inflation relative to public debt to GDP ratio (%), 1946-08

Figure 37. *Source: Reinhart and Rogoff*

And as we also explained before, the IMF found that economic recovery after a recession was significantly weaker for countries that had public debt ratios above 60% of GDP than for those below[2]. And Carmen Reinhart and Kenneth Rogoff published an analysis of the impact on economic growth of rising levels of public sector debt for the top 20 advanced economies from 1946-09[3]. They show that once government debt to/GDP levels in advanced economies exceed 90%, economies tend to suffer notably lower growth outcomes. In addition, for emerging markets, there appears to be a more stringent threshold for total external debt/GDP (60%) that is also associated with adverse outcomes for growth and inflation as well.

Reinhart & Rogoff found that, as public sector debt reached 90% of GDP or over, it would cut average real GDP growth by 1.0-1.5% pts compared to growth rates achieved when public sector debt was lower. Emerging economies also suffered sharply rising inflation as debt increased (Figure 37).

The consequence of adding public sector leverage to excessive private sector credit will be to push economic growth below trend at best and may even create stagnation, Japanese-style. It will not boost growth as the Keynesian identities suggest.

Government dissaving leads to increased public debt. And public debts have significant financial and real economic consequences. The recent sharp rise in risk premia on long-term bonds issued by several industrial countries suggests that markets no longer consider sovereign debt low-risk. Default risk premia will move up with debt levels. Countries with a relatively weak fiscal system and a high degree of dependence on foreign investors to finance their deficits generally face much larger spreads on their debts.

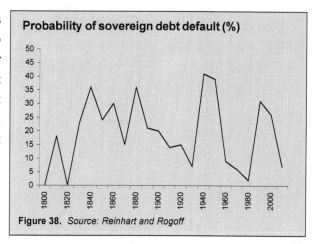

Probability of sovereign debt default (%)

Figure 38. *Source: Reinhart and Rogoff*

Persistently high levels of public debt will also drive down capital accumulation, productivity gains and potential growth. And looming long-term fiscal imbalances also pose significant risk to the prospects for future monetary stability. Finally, the history of sovereign debt defaults reveals that they come in waves like earthquakes (Figure 38). There has been a lull in the past few years. So we could be due for a new wave. In that sense, this time will probably not be different.

1. World Bank op cit.

2. IMF WEO op cit.

3. Reinhart and Rogoff, *The forgotten history of domestic debt,* April 2008.

CHAPTER SIX

The globalisation of sovereign debt

The difference between Reinhart and Rogoff's historical analysis of individual countries in crisis and today's situation is that so many large economies are now in crisis together and must draw on a common pool of international savings to finance themselves as never before.

If you owe debt to your family, you are less vulnerable than if you owe it to someone else. In the case of sovereign debt, the country that funds its sovereign debt from domestic sources is less vulnerable to a sovereign debt crisis than would be the case if it owed the money to foreigners.

Italy is a case in point. By any standards, its state was bust for decades. But its citizens had massive savings which they mostly invested in government bonds at high yields (in pre-euro days). There was little need for financing from abroad.

Today, however, thanks to the globalisation of capital markets, most highly-indebted countries owe a significant proportion of their debts to foreigners as they have inadequate domestic savings to finance their growing stock of government debt (Figure 39).

The factors that allow a country to domesticate its sovereign liabilities can be boiled down to: a) a high savings rate matched by investor preference for investing in 'low risk' government debt of

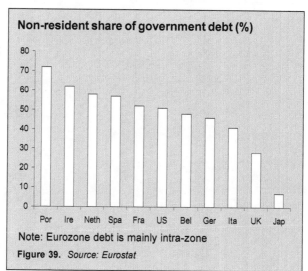

Non-resident share of government debt (%)

Note: Eurozone debt is mainly intra-zone

Figure 39. *Source: Eurostat*

their own government; b) a current account surplus, denoting surplus domestic savings to investment needs; which can bolster the domestic currency and flatter domestic bond performance; and c) low foreign ownership of domestic debt.

If these factors are of long duration, so will be the domestication of sovereign debt. If they are merely marginal and cyclical phenomena, the ability to domesticate debt will be temporary. A cyclical domestication of debt could be possible if a current account balance improves, and if household savings rise and consumption falls temporarily during a recession (Figure 40).

Distinguishing between the temporary and durable types of domestication of sovereign debt is what sets a government's ability to increase its debt beyond reasonable levels of GDP without engendering a sovereign debt crisis. Japan and Italy succeeded in doing this for decades. But what about the newcomers on the scene, like the UK and US, which have managed to stave off a sovereign debt crisis so far by domesticating their vast issuance of sovereign debt during this crisis?

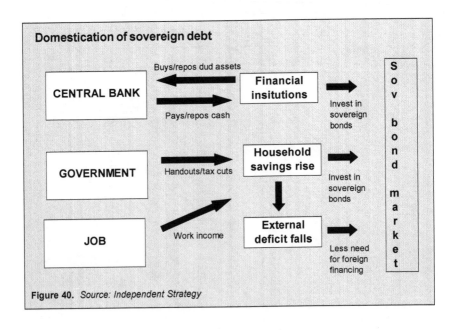

Figure 40. *Source: Independent Strategy*

The build-up of excessive sovereign debt has partly been funded by a rise in household savings. Households became highly risk-averse in the aftermath of the credit crisis and were hunting better yields than cash deposits. So they bought more government bonds.

At the same time, central banks stepped up the purchase of government debt through specific 'quantitative easing' programmes. They also bought dud assets from the banks as part of financial sector bailout schemes and the banks used the proceeds from such sales to buy government debt rather than lend to the 'real' economy. All these factors together made the rise in sovereign leverage financeable in the short term without increased recourse to foreign savers.

Finally, the US current account deficit, one of the great global imbalances, shrank because consumers were saving more and spending less, thus reducing imports and the need for more foreign financing.

However, this domestication of increasing sovereign leverage is fragile and temporary and will come to an end when central banks remove the special measures that have created exceptional demand for sovereign bonds; when consumption expands, causing household savings rates to fall and the current account deficit to deepen; and when household risk appetite increases and individual investors turn away from bonds to equities.

The US government will then either have to cut debt issuance by raising taxation and slashing discretionary spending, or it will have to rely on foreigners to buy more treasuries. If it is the latter, then foreigners will want higher yields as the dollar is no longer in play as a trusted reserve currency.

Indeed, although the US current account deficit has shrunk during the economic recession, the external financing gap — the difference between the current account deficit and private foreign capital inflows — has hardly

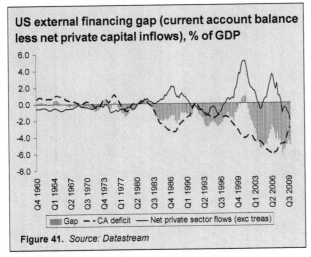

Figure 41. *Source: Datastream*

Figure 42. *Source: Datastream*

narrowed at all because foreigners cut back on their purchases of dollar assets (Figure 41).

The main funders of US government debt issuance remain foreigners. Foreign holdings constitute nearly half of all outstanding US sovereign debt (Figure 42).

The key foreign savers and buyers of US dollar assets, Japan and China, look increasingly hesitant to cover even existing US financing needs.

Already, psychologically, the pricing of the US dollar is no longer based on its role as the global reserve currency of choice, although quantitatively it is still the biggest reserve currency, of course.

Japan has its own fiscal crisis to deal with and could well use its huge stock of foreign assets to do so — as we shall see in a future chapter. The Japanese could choose to repatriate the 12% of marketable US government debt owned by the government to fund Japan's own unsustain-

able public fi-
nances. The pen-
alty would be a
rapid collapse of
the greenback and
sharply higher US
long-term bond
yields.

That would put an
end to the treasury
bond bubble and to
the dollar as the
dominant global re-
serve currency.

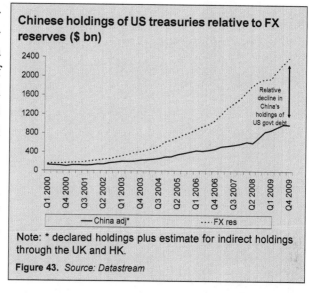

Chinese holdings of US treasuries relative to FX reserves ($ bn)

Relative decline in China's holdings of US govt debt

— China adj*   ···· FX res

Note: * declared holdings plus estimate for indirect holdings through the UK and HK.

Figure 43. *Source: Datastream*

However this plays out, faced with rising demands to finance US profligacy, it is unlikely that the Japanese and the Chinese will play ball indefi-
nitely. Indeed, there is evidence that China is consistently moving to diversify its assets out of dollars in general, and US treasuries in particular,
if so far in only a gradual manner (Figure 43).

CHAPTER SEVEN

Europe's debt crisis

Is Greece the 'sub-prime' starting point of the global sovereign credit crisis? Numerous are the differences between Greece, Spain, Portugal and Ireland — almost as numerous as the differences between sub-prime and prime mortgages. But there was, and is, one common denominator — excessive leverage in the public sector (Figure 44).

Excessive leverage becomes a credit crisis when the liquidity to fund it dries up. Credit is liquidity. Liquidity dries up when the stock of excessive credit can't renew itself. Then the stock can't be rolled over. So it has to shrink.

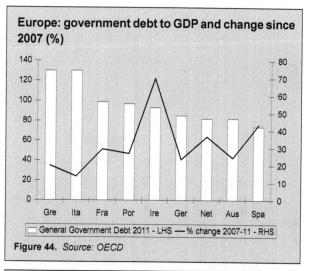

Europe: government debt to GDP and change since 2007 (%)

General Government Debt 2011 - LHS — % change 2007-11 - RHS

Figure 44. *Source: OECD*

Public sector leverage is becoming unsustainable (Figure 45). That is the common denominator for Greece and the other over-leveraged states. How they got there is irrelevant. They all have arrived at the same destina-

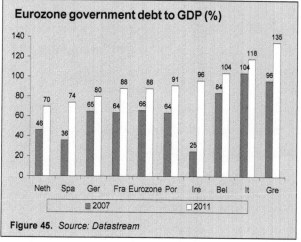

Eurozone government debt to GDP (%)

2007   2011

Figure 45. *Source: Datastream*

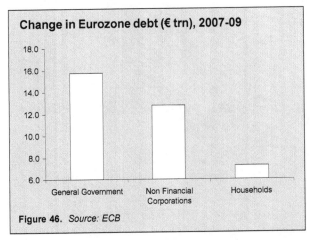

Change in Eurozone debt (€ trn), 2007-09

Figure 46. *Source: ECB*

tion. So the consequences will be the same — a sovereign credit squeeze when liquidity dries up.

As we have argued, it is baloney that policy makers *swapped* public for private sector debt to combat the credit crisis. They actually *added* public sector leverage to an almost unaltered level of private sector debt to create super leverage. That applies to Europe too (Figure 46).

Also EU countries have almost doubled their amount of short-term debt since 2007, to about 11% of the total outstanding. Clearly, it can make tactical sense to borrow at near-zero interest rates, but rolling over such debts, worth more than €800bn in 2010, also increases the chances of a blow-up. The UK must roll over debt worth 5% of output this year but Spain must roll over 12% and Greece 13%. Belgium, Italy and Ireland, at about 20% apiece, have an even bigger task.

Why did this EMU sovereign credit crisis not happen sooner? Because for a crisis to happen, sovereign leverage has to be allowed to build to unsustainable levels *and* liquidity has to dry up. In other words, markets have to become aware that the absolute level of sovereign debt is unfinanceable. That level of unsustainability has already been reached in many minor and major economies. The markets are only just becoming aware of this as the spread on interest-rate swaps reveals (Figure 47).

Bond spreads between Germany and the weaker Euro states have widened reflecting the poorer fundamentals of these countries. However, the nominal cost of their government debt has hardly shifted because of declining long rates globally. With the exception of Greece, most EU governments are paying now much the same rate as they paid before (Figure 48).

The cost for these weaker Eurozone countries is only the opportunity cost of not having cheaper German debt.

Some argue that the euro is about to break up under the stress of the global credit crunch and an impending sovereign debt crisis.

The reasons the euro will survive are manifold. The euro (together with the other EU institutions) is all about

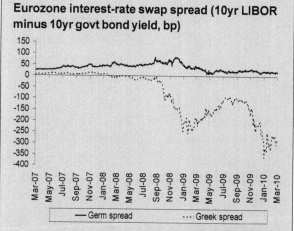

Eurozone interest-rate swap spread (10yr LIBOR minus 10yr govt bond yield, bp)

Interest-rate swap spreads reflect the shift in risk recognised by markets between private sector and public sector debt. The spread is the gap between the fixed interest-rate and the yield on the government bond of the same maturity. They are usually positive because markets expect governments to be able to borrow at a cheaper rate than the private sector. The German swap spread is still positive, but has declined in the last three years; the Greek spread is hugely negative.

Figure 47. *Source: Datastream*

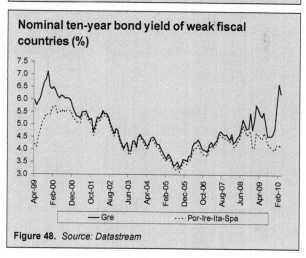

Nominal ten-year bond yield of weak fiscal countries (%)

Figure 48. *Source: Datastream*

history, not economics. It is the instrument that consummated the dilution of German nationalism into the European identity. By reverse osmosis, the EU and the euro are guarantors that keep Italian politicians mildly clean-handed and for the Portuguese, Spanish and Greeks that their regimes became democratic. The cement of history is a lot stronger than that of economics. Even in times of recession, popular support for the euro is unlikely to fall to the level where populist politicians could muster enough support to leave.

Convergence with the Eurozone gives the peripheral countries of Europe a cost of capital that is way cheaper than that dictated by their weaker fundamentals (such as government debts and deficits and competitiveness). Leaving the euro would destroy them. First, there would be a run on their banks as depositors sought to get euros in cash. Second, there would be a big devaluation of whatever currencies they introduced to replace the euro with. But the euro would remain the currency in which their liabilities were denominated, so the cost of their debt would go through the roof. Finally, a country leaving the euro is legally obliged to leave the EU. These factors alone would completely negate any benefits to be gained from devaluation and increased competitiveness.

Currency unions only break up when the strong core backers, not the weak peripheral dependents, walk out and stop paying. For reasons of history, Germany is about as likely to walk out as it is to invade Poland again. Germany is unlikely to give up on the euro provided it can set the fiscal and monetary policy rules to maintain it as a strong currency.

After all, the Eurozone works. Its haphazard structure seems to eschew the political and economic excesses of more focused regimes. The EU is wealthy, civilised and secular. So, like families of similar condition, it is well able to withstand shocks and the odd black sheep.

In the current credit crisis, the Central European states were either bankrupted or bailed out before they became so. Ireland, which had a credit bubble to end all credit bubbles, survived more or less intact because it had no currency for speculators to attack and because it could decide how to bail out its own banks without too much interference from the Brussels bureaucracy (post-facto criticism hardly counts!).

By complete accident, Europe had the right structure to deal with credit crises: subsidiarity of decision-making to the national level when dealing with financial restructuring; and a single currency that protects individual states from speculative attack. This has been spotted by the European states that are not members of the Eurozone. Hence the rush by Central European countries to get into the euro.

When push comes to shove, all Eurozone countries will be ring-fenced to prevent any domestic credit crisis becoming a sovereign debt default. Of course, the Germans will exact a price for their backstopping of the euro. They will impose their vision of what needs to be done to combat credit crises upon other member states. Fiscal stringency and strict and minimal bailouts will be the rule.

Germany can impose its economic model upon its peers because it has emerged from the crisis as a bedrock of stability in the Eurozone. In the recession, its economy has suffered much from the decline in demand for its capital goods and vehicles, but the economic model is unquestioned by its people. Its financial system, despite the Anglo-Saxon media's prediction of its impending collapse, is relatively unscathed and has been in less need of Anglo-Saxon-sized bailouts.

That is not to say that the German leadership judged the crisis well or did everything right. German Chancellor, Angela Merkel, misjudged the financial crisis completely and opposed a Europe-wide bank restructuring plan when it was most needed. Her performance on Greece has been hesitant, arguably devoid of any European vision and entailed second-guessing the markets. Her government's proposal to purchase Germany's bad bank assets without marking them to market was typical of policy makers seeking to prolong denial. Her government's backing of the Opel deal was a beggar-thy-neighbour, job-preserving case study in bad policy.

But, as so often in the case of the Eurozone, Germany has the stability of a jellyfish — when kicked, it wobbles and continues on as before. It is a form of stability that is partly down to the limitations of a democratic

Germany and the Eurozone

Some argue that the Eurozone debt crisis will destroy the credibility of the euro. The argument goes: Germany wants the likes of Greece, Portugal, Spain and Ireland to be like Germany; no fiscal deficits and no external deficits. But to have that means ending Germany's current account surplus and its ability to grow through exports. Germany will have to spend domestically or the Eurozone will stay stagnant for years as the high-deficit, high debt EMU states will be in a permanent slump. Germany will have nowhere to export to.

It's true that 50% of Germany's exports go to the Eurozone, but German exports to Greece and Iberia are nowhere near as large as exports to other Eurozone countries like France and Benelux, or to eastern Europe, Asia (China) and the US. So, although there could be a marginal reduction in Germany's net trade surplus while the Greeks and the Spaniards suffer a slump, economic growth and increased demand for German goods elsewhere will more than compensate.

Figure 49. *Source: Independent Strategy*

system founded on coalition politics and by a federal constitution. German politicians can't do big things — either wise or foolish.

It is a stability that, in economic terms, is bolstered by the Germans' simple vision of sticking to what they are good at — making superbly engineered products desired by all the world. The Germans just make them better and better as the rest of the world moves on to enrich itself with other things, like *financial* engineering! In a world in dire need of such stability, this is a priceless asset (Figure 49).

Moreover, Germany is the only country in the world with an exit strategy from the current explosion in government debts and deficits — one that is now set in constitutional stone. Germany has now made fiscal stability a priority policy goal. It has enshrined the virtual elimination of structural budget deficits in its constitution.

This is a fiscal stability law that surpasses even such fiscally-virtuous places as New Zealand. And because it is written in stone, it will happen (Figure 50).

Germany now wants to replace Jean-Claude Trichet as president of the ECB with a German, when his current term ends in November 2011. In this way, they plan to control both monetary and fiscal policy in the Eurozone. Germany also wants a new tough set of rules and reporting requirements to apply to all Euro members and applicants. Violating

---

German fiscal law

From 2016, it will be illegal for the federal government to run a structural deficit of more than 0.35% of GDP. From 2020, the Länder will not be allowed to run any deficits at all. It means that future fiscal policy will be in the hands of the German constitutional court.

The so-called budget ceiling amendment forces the government to start reducing its federal budget deficit from 2011. There are only two possible variations from this course under the law: 1) "exceptional circumstances" and 2) varying the pace of the reduction in the deficit from 2011 to 2016. The German government has the leeway to accelerate or reduce the level of the cuts as it wishes over the years until 2016, provided it still meets the target by 2016.

Because the budget requirement is now in the constitution, its interpretation falls to the Constitutional Court. The Court is famous for taking a very restrictive interpretation of the constitution. It is virtually certain, for instance, that the Court will interpret the "exceptional circumstances" clause in the constitutional amendment in a very narrow way, namely an economic crisis which is 'very grave'. So no regular economic downturns would be considered as applicable. Furthermore, the Court will also view the exception as a one-off event, requiring any future government to adhere to the budget deficit ceiling.

Figure 50. *Source: Independent Strategy*

---

them could even lead to expulsion! Not complying with them on a sustainable basis rules out joining. Whether this becomes part of a new Maastricht Treaty or not, it is how things will be run.

Sure, the Merkel government is increasing fiscal thrust by 2% pts of GDP in 2010. Her strategy is to kick-start the economy and then rein in government spending structurally. Not being a fool, she knows that enforcing the new no-deficit fiscal rules will be a lot easier in a growing economy than a stagnating or shrinking one.

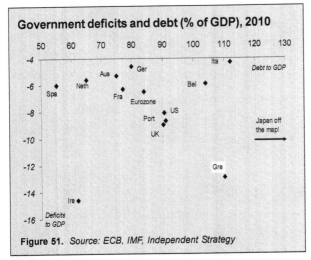

Figure 51. Source: ECB, IMF, Independent Strategy

A look around the Eurozone shows Germany in splendid and virtuous fiscal isolation, near the bottom of the debt and deficit matrix (Figure 51).

Suppose the Germans were the only Eurozone country to achieve a structurally balanced budget. France, despite the 3% of GDP budget deficit rule set by the Maastricht treaty, intends to run deficits of 5-7% each year up to 2012. Greece, Ireland, Spain and nearly all the rest have worse deficits.

Could Germany allow such sustained fiscal divergence to happen? It would mean Germany would experience fiscal austerity, while everyone else had a party. Politically and economically, that is impossible. Politically, the Germans would simply refuse to pay for it. Economically, the real exchange rate of Germany versus the partying countries would diverge at an alarming rate. Ultimately, the euro would be doomed.

The key battlefield for the divergent role of the state and the condition of public finances will be between Germany and France. French president Sarkozy knows on which side of the euro his economy is buttered. France will fall into line and the weak perimeter countries will have no choice but to do likewise. If they refuse, their days in the euro will be numbered and the bond and credit default markets will complete their massacre.

Ironically, bond markets are the doomsday machine that will whip the fiscally profligate states into line. There is no policy option to do so, as there is no clause in the Maastricht treaty that allows for ejection of member states that run a lousy economic ship. This is one thing Germany rightly wants to change. It is possible that as a result of the Greek crisis such clauses will be the subject of a new treaty. But for now, the markets will do the job instead.

Fiscal austerity will eventually impart a big growth dividend to the Eurozone. There is no way to reduce structural budget deficits and excessive levels of government debt by increasing taxes anywhere in the Eurozone. The job has to be done by shrinking the role of the state, particularly in areas related to social security and the workforce.

European governments spend close to 50 cents out of every euro of national income (Figure 52). That is obviously bad value. So it is spending that has to come down, not taxation up.

If governments were to spend less, the private sector could spend more — and more productively, creating more wealth. When the state spends more, people save more and spend less. The tendency for people to do so grows, as the public debt to GDP ratio rises. They know the state has no money of its own and thus public spending now simply means that the politicians will take it away from the electorate in taxes or reduced public services later.

The same works in reverse. For the money that the state stops spending does not create a vacuum, but an opportunity. If the state spends less, other economic agents will spend more and better.

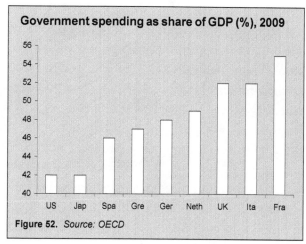

Government spending as share of GDP (%), 2009

Figure 52. *Source: OECD*

Moreover, the state's withdrawal from specific sectors creates opportunities for others to fill real needs (e.g. running crèches when parents go to work, rather than living and breeding on unemployment benefit). Finally, the retreat of the state also shrinks its legislative reach over the economy and, in particular, over work practices. This empowers the setting-up of small entrepreneurial companies unencumbered by restrictive labour and other laws.

In Germany's case, this could be the virtuous way in which its services industry gets developed and the economy's export dependence is reduced. This is all grist to the mill of those who think the resolution of global imbalances has to be through less saving and more consumer spending in the excess savings and current account surplus countries of the world. But the way to achieve this in Germany is not through fiscal handouts to the consumer, which would be saved not spent, but by structural reforms that shrink the role of the state.

The creation of a more dynamic Eurozone economy can be empowered only by the downsizing of the state. And that, inadvertently or maybe just intelligently, is what Germany has set in motion for the whole Eurozone by enshrining fiscal responsibility in its constitution.

Eastern Europe's euro dilemma

The exposure to foreign financing of debt is particularly acute in Europe. EMU states like Greece and Portugal depend on German, Swiss and Dutch banks to buy their debt issuance. And we have seen how that has mushroomed into a major debt crisis which is still unfolding as Eurozone governments seek to refinance their debt (Figure 53).

But the situation is much more serious in the several countries in central and eastern Europe aspiring to join the Eurozone (Hungary, Romania, the Baltics) and others further afield in emerging Europe, like Turkey, Ukraine and the Balkans.

The lack of domestication of debt has been at the core of the credit crisis in central and eastern Europe (Figure 54). In Eastern Europe, the debt problem initially concerned foreign debt taken on by the private sector. Many countries have massive foreign liabilities, much in the form of Swiss franc and euro-denominated bank lending to domestic households used to buy cars and houses. And this has been made worse by incurring more foreign debt

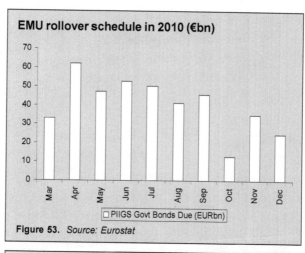

Figure 53. *Source: Eurostat*

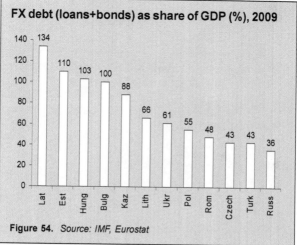

Figure 54. *Source: IMF, Eurostat*

in the form of loans from the IMF to prevent a foreign debt crisis gaining traction in 2009, as well as by a strong Swiss franc.

Government debt prices among all the EMU aspirants in central and southeastern Europe are potentially vulnerable to a tightening of the application of the Maastricht criteria for entry into the single currency.

As a consequence of the Greek crisis, EMU convergence criteria are going to be strictly applied to all new euro candidates and the qualifying data minutely will be audited. The criteria will be stress-tested for sustainability in the future and there will be no monkey business with derivative swaps as in the case of Greece. This means that most of these EMU aspirants, particularly Hungary, Romania, Bulgaria and the Baltics, will not have any chance of euro membership before 2015 at the earliest (Figure 55).

Given that euro membership is now more remote, emerging Europe's foreign-currency debt will be now more vulnerable for much longer. Most will require annual rollover rates of 100% of their foreign debt burden in 2010 to stay the course. If a crisis starts, it will quickly reduce risk appetite and affect other emerging markets. The risk of a major debt crisis in emerging Europe will remain until these countries gain access to the Eurozone.

EMU convergence criteria at 2011 — only Estonia would qualify now					
	ERMII	Interest rate (%)	CPI (%)	Govt deficit (% GDP)	Govt debt (% GDP)	Total met
Reference level	2yrs	6.2	2.5	3	60	5
Bulgaria	no	no	no	yes	yes	2
Czech Republic	no	yes	yes	no	yes	3
Estonia	Jun'04	yes	yes	yes	yes	5
Latvia	May'05	no	yes	no	no	1
Lithuania	Jun'04	no	yes	no	yes	2
Hungary	no	no	yes	no	no	1
Poland	no	yes	yes	no	yes	3
Romania	no	no	no	no	yes	1

Figure 55. *Source: EU Commission*

CHAPTER EIGHT

Japan's debt miracle

Today, Japan's gross public debt stands around 200% of GDP and its net debt is 130% of GDP , according to our estimates (Figure 56). Both figures dwarf its OECD peers. How did Japan get there? And how has it done so without a sovereign debt crisis?

Japan is living proof that government deficit spending, high public debt and central bank liquidity largesse do not result in a vibrant economy. If it were true, Japan would be the most dynamic economy in the world.

A realistic estimate of Japan's public debt

Japan's gross government debt ratio is by far the highest in the OECD, reaching 202% at end-2009, or nearly double the OECD average. However, some argue that Japan's sovereign debt problem is overdone because the government has considerable financial and non-financial assets that ought to be taken into account.

If the government's financial assets are fully deducted, then net government debt would fall to 103% of GDP. If the government balance sheet is adjusted for the liabilities of public pension funds, along with contingent liabilities or guarantees not listed as liabilities and financial assets that probably cannot be sold, net debt would rise from 103% to 166% of GDP.

However, it is also possible that non-financial assets (public land and properties) could be sold and, indeed, the Japanese government does have plans to do that. That could reduce net debt to about 140% of GDP. Finally, it is possible that some of Japan's official holdings of foreign-currency assets worth about 12% of GDP could be sold off. So the net debt level could be considered closer to 130% of GDP. That is still greater than Greece's gross public sector debt ratio expected in 2011.

Japan's public sector balance sheet (% of GDP)

	Q4'07	Q4'08	Q2'09	Q3'09	Q4'09
Total financial assets	**98**	**97**	**97**	**98**	**99**
Currency and deposits	9	8	8	8	8
Deposits with the Fiscal Loan Fund	14	11	10	10	10
Loans	5	5	5	6	6
Securities other than shares	24	27	27	27	26
Shares and other equities	19	18	19	19	20
Outward investment	24	22	23	23	24
Other	4	5	5	5	5
Total liabilities	**183**	**190**	**198**	**202**	**206**
Loans	36	36	36	36	37
Securities other than shares	139	147	155	159	162
Shares and other equity	3	3	4	4	4
Other	4	4	4	4	3

Figure 56. *Source: Independent Strategy*

When Japan's credit bubble burst in 1989, Japan's household savings rate was over 15% of disposable income. And Japan still has the largest stock of household savings per capita in the world, four times that of US households. Then, as now, about two-thirds of those savings were accumulated by people over 55 years old. These old folk, being risk averse, put two-thirds of their savings in bank and post office deposits at vile interest rates (a 0.1% p.a. deposit rate was the norm!).

But why did Japanese savers accept such terrible returns on so much hard-earned savings? Of course, the Japanese weren't stupid at all. The post-bubble collapse meant consumer prices fell to zero from 3% per year. This stopped any significant erosion of the real value of their savings, even with meagre interest receipts.

Moreover, real and nominal wages in Japan continued to rise and job creation continued apace because the social contract prevented labour markets from functioning as all sensible free-market models say they should (Figure 57)!

Bank deposits initially fell after the bubble burst, but then rose steadily. In their lost decade(s), that terrible era of 'deflation' that the US authorities now fight (valiantly) to save us all from once again, the Japanese got progressively richer and kept their jobs.

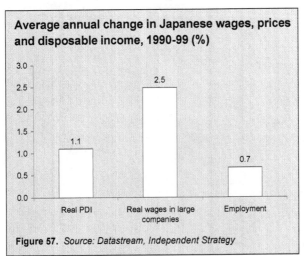

Average annual change in Japanese wages, prices and disposable income, 1990-99 (%)

Figure 57. *Source: Datastream, Independent Strategy*

Through the nineties, the BoJ also supplied limitless additional free money, which the bankers added to household deposits and, having no borrowers worth lending to, they invested the lot in Japanese government bonds (JGBs). This yielded a risk-free (almost infinite) rate of return to the banks, as the cost of the borrowed money was almost zilch and they had to use almost none of their own capital.

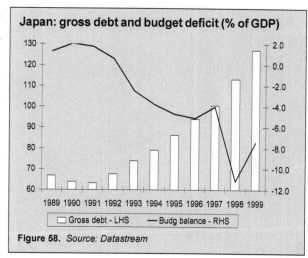

Japan: gross debt and budget deficit (% of GDP)

Gross debt - LHS — Budg balance - RHS

Figure 58. *Source: Datastream*

Such massive inflows into JGBs caused JGB prices to rise and made yields incredibly low. This is what saved the government from bankruptcy. And that's saying something when, in the years of post-bubble fiscal profligacy, the budget deficit blew out to 10% of GDP and gross debt to GDP topped 120% (Figure 58).

Comparisons get even more extreme if a little currency adjustment is introduced. For the whole of the post-bubble period (1990-99), expressed in the common currency of the yen, ten-year JGB returns averaged 6% p.a. compared to less than 1% in yen for US treasuries. And the yen value of Japanese household wealth increased by 25% compared to 20% for US households.

If economies are there to serve the people, the Japanese economy did a damned good job for one supposedly hovering on the brink of oft-foretold collapse. In fact, come to think of it, for dyed-in-the-wool apostles of the free market, it is galling that two of the world's richest economies, Germany and Japan, emerged from the ashes of war to become wealthy, clean, civic, honest, polite and a few other pleasant things, with scant reference to our 'market-knows-best' econoculture.

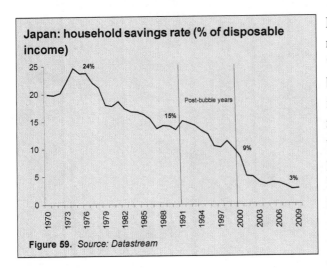

Japan: household savings rate (% of disposable income)

Figure 59. *Source: Datastream*

But Japan cannot now repeat the 'miracle' of going broke and not being penalised. The reason this will not work again in Japan is that the household savings rate has now collapsed to 3% (Figure 59), or less than the US equivalent. So, if the Japanese government is now going to run budget deficits at double-digit percentage rates of GDP, it can no longer draw on low-cost household savings to do so.

The household savings rate is unlikely to rise because it is demography (the need to spend to finance old age) that is the main reason for its fall. Thus Japan's low saving rate is something death must undo, not the politicians or monetary policy.

"Ah", you may say, "but what about the huge stock of Japanese household savings?" To understand why that doesn't do the trick, it is necessary to distinguish between stocks and flows. The total aggregation of savings accumulated over the years is a stock. The money added to it every year is a flow. Similarly, outstanding government debt is a stock and the budget deficit is a flow.

Sure, Mrs Watanabe has more savings than her international peers. But those savings are already invested, through financial intermediaries such as banks and life insurance companies, in the stock of existing JGBs that keep the politicians afloat in the sea of their own incompetence.

The stock of savings can be used to roll over existing government debts. A maturing JGB is paid off and the proceeds then get reinvested in a new JGB that replaces the old one. But the budget deficit has still got to be financed. The budget deficit is a (negative) new flow and has to be financed with a (positive) flow of new savings. And it is this flow of new savings that is lacking.

The other domestic sources of funding for the government debt are the postal savings (JP), postal insurance and public pension funds (GPIF). These institutions are unable to step up to the plate as their assets are diminishing and they are stuffed with JGBs already. Together, these three institutions hold about 44% of all JGBs. Given declining assets, their JGB holdings are likely to shrink, not expand (Figure 60).

It has been argued that Japan still has a high corporate savings rate (17% of GDP) and that corporations could invest in JGBs. Corporations may have plenty of savings. But they don't use them to invest in government bonds, but in their own businesses. Corporate bank deposits are only one-fifth the size of household deposits. So any realistic increase in corporate purchases would not

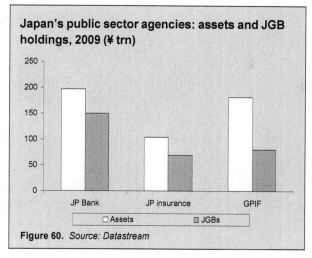

Figure 60. *Source: Datastream*

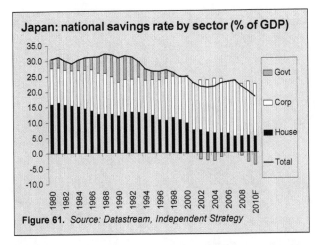

Figure 61. *Source: Datastream, Independent Strategy*

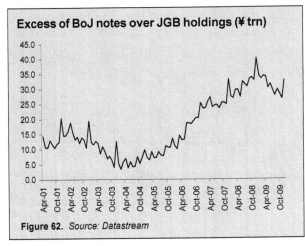

Figure 62. *Source: Datastream*

be enough to compensate for falling household savings and slowing growth of household bank deposits (Figure 61).

The Bank of Japan (BoJ) is the buyer of last resort for JGBs and, in theory, has unlimited capacity to expand its balance sheet to buy JGBs. But the BoJ tries to limit its JGB holdings to cash in circulation. To hold more JGBs, it either has to print more money or change its rules.

Assuming that the current growth rate of the monetary base is not altered, the BoJ can only add about ¥30trn to its current holdings of about ¥27trn (Figure 62).

Compare that to planned total JGB market issuance in this next fiscal year, 2010-11, of ¥136trn (net new of ¥50trn) and more in subsequent years. As a result, the private sector (including foreigners) must add a minimum of 10% per year to their JGB holdings to meet government borrowing requirements.

The amazing paradigm of the post-bubble years, when the twin surpluses of excess domestic savings and the basic balance of payments kept the yen rising, government deficits sated and public funding costs at rock bottom, cannot be repeated. Now Japan will have to attract foreign capital to balance both its external account and its government books.

It is a stretch to believe that foreign savers will jump at the opportunity to fund an insolvent government at the lowest government bond yields in the world. So a great repricing of JGBs will be caused by the inevitable participation of foreign buyers as price setters — something completely new to a JGB bond market that has always been predominantly domestically-owned.

Japan now has a public debt ratio that is nearly as twice as bad as that of Greece, where government debt yields are more than double that of Germany, despite having the same currency and an implicit Eurozone bailout guarantee. All this means that Japan's JGB yields will eventually have to converge with German or US yields and even establish a healthy yield premium to them.

Japan's basic balance of payments deficit is the final great break with the past (Figure 63). It means that the yen will be a weak currency. This diminishes the attractiveness of JGBs for both international and domestic investors.

Moreover, the external funding of the budget deficit and debt rollovers will have to be achieved against the backdrop of competition for savings from other OECD govern-

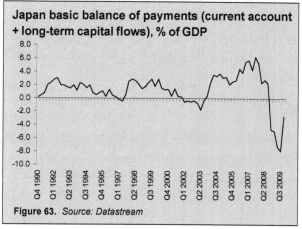

Figure 63. *Source: Datastream*

ments which all together need to raise $8trn a year (including rollovers), or nearly 20% of OECD GDP. With the yen doomed by its own deficit arithmetic to being a weak currency, there is no way this can be done at yields 200bp below Germany!

To stop the long-term upward trajectory of public sector debt to GDP and get the ratio back to international levels, Japan needs to run a primary budget surplus of 8% of GDP a year for over a decade compared to a primary deficit today of 4%. Such a massive deflationary fiscal shift is very unlikely under a DPJ government that seeks to expand government spending rather than shrink it.

In the case of a Japanese sovereign debt crisis, the Japanese private sector would not repatriate its share of foreign assets to fund a domestic sovereign debt crisis. Indeed, private sector flows would be the other way — out.

Japan could sell some of its public assets to pay down debt. After all, Japan is the largest international creditor nation in world, the result of years of recycling large current account surpluses. A considerable slice of Japan's foreign assets is owned by government and could be brought home to reduce public debt or in order to fund budget deficits. The government owns foreign assets worth 12% of GDP, mainly in the form of US government marketable debt. We reckon that Japan could sell or repatriate state assets sufficient to fund one year's budget deficit or reduce its gross sovereign debt burden by 6% at most. And the trouble is that this could take a long time to realise, while Japan's deficit and debt continue to grow.

If Japan sold its holdings of US treasuries, it could lead to a collapse in US bond prices that could sweep across global bond markets. It could also cause the yen to rise, although the Japanese could lessen the impact by printing yen to swap for the repatriated dollars and by not sterilising the newly distributed yen afterwards. But the sum that could be realised from foreign asset sales is not enough to make a long-term difference to

Japan. And selling US treasuries would set off a diplomatic furore as Japan would be seen to be pursuing a beggar-thy-neighbour policy that would further strengthen the hand of China on the geopolitical stage.

Because sovereign debt has become globalised, any attempt to sell public assets, particularly ones held abroad, would have major repercussions for other countries with high levels of sovereign debt. Japan's sovereign debt crisis could spread contagion.

CHAPTER NINE

China's credit bubble

The Chinese have a sovereign credit crisis too, but with one difference: their debt is domesticated to a high degree; they owe it to themselves. Indeed, the state both lends and borrows much of the credits between different branches of itself. This can prolong the life of its bubble. Much of the bad credit and dud assets that will surface when the bubble bursts will be owed and owned by the state itself.

China's growth 'miracle' in 2009 was really a product of massive fiscal and monetary stimulus ordered by government *dictat* (Figure 64). A Rmb4trn ($600bn) fiscal stimulus programme, of which relatively little was actually spent, was supported by a rise of over Rmb9trn ($1.3trn) in new bank loans used to boost investment and infrastructure.

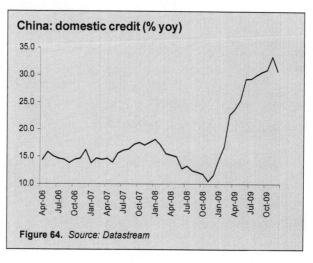

Figure 64. *Source: Datastream*

Last year, total fixed-asset investment accounted for more than 90% of China's overall GDP growth; residential and commercial real estate investment comprised nearly a quarter of that. Now the signs of overheating are becoming obvious, even in the view of the Chinese authorities. Imports are now rising at a much faster pace than expected as China continues to suck in commodities. Inflation is accelerating. At the same time, the property boom is out of control with investment in real estate outstripping even government infrastructure spending. China is awash with liquidity that is fuelling asset bubbles.

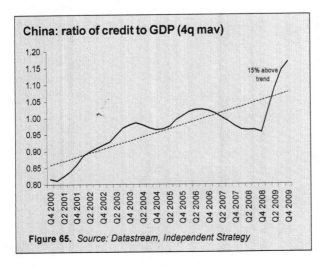

Figure 65. *Source: Datastream, Independent Strategy*

Much of the injection of liquidity went into stockpiling commodities and raw materials, additional overcapacity in industry and a real estate bubble. Increased productivity, which would sustain good economic growth without inflation and overheating, was missing. Indeed, the incremental increase in credit relative to GDP growth (Figure 65) has reached record proportions, revealing a sharp fall in capital productivity.

There are those who argue that this lending explosion merely reflects the democratisation of credit in China. If so, it's the only thing that is being democratised! With consumer credit at a low 17% of GDP, even in this bubble, that theory seems a stretch.

China has one enormous monetary policy advantage: Beijing still controls the banks, even though it no longer owns all of them. This is the serendipity of an incompletely-reformed, centrally-planned economy. Beijing can dictate to the banks what to lend and to whom. Non-compliance can be a nasty experience.

By comparison, pity poor Mr. Bernanke. He can only ask the banks to take his (Fed) money *gratis*, but cannot control what they do with it. This happens to be precious little when it comes to extending credit to the real economy. Mr. Bernanke's control of credit stops at the door of the commercial banks.

In contrast, Beijing controls the whole credit distribution chain. All bubbles need credit creation. Beijing can make it happen. Therefore, the Chinese are more effective when it comes to starting bubbles. But even they cannot control everything. No banker can control what happens to loans when the stock is expanding at over 30% yoy. Our bankers couldn't, — so theirs, who are less experienced, can't either. Although credit may be extended to one entity for one purpose, it may fund something entirely different. Money, after all, is fungible.

It isn't as though China suffers from undeveloped bank credit either. Bank credit to GDP in China is 130% compared to India 55%, Brazil 50% and Russia 50%. So a 10% increase in lending in China amounts to 13% of GDP in new credit and half that in most other emerging markets.

The Chinese circuitry is simple. In one way, it is more of a Japanese-style bubble, with banks lending madly to corporations, rather than to individuals, but with an added locomotive of government dictating the whole process and adding power in the form of fiscal stimulus.

Ordered to lend, the banks have complied. And they had good reason (other than fear) to do so. Their loan to deposit ratio had fallen way below their credit capacity due to the previous policy of credit tightening. And their interest-rate margins were declining. As they had just been 'privatised', they needed to lend more to grow profits and get their share prices up.

You will recognise that this is the same behaviour pattern that characterised our Western banks during the credit bubble. Individual banks optimised their performance and sub-optimised the common good by jeopardising the stability of the entire credit system.

The Chinese bankers started out by lending to their old mates: the state-owned enterprises (SOEs) — the sink hole where they had previously run up a pile of bad debts, with which the system is still struggling. That sink soon filled. The SOEs took all the money they could and ploughed it into 'productive' investments, like speculating on their own raw materials (hence the boom in industrial commodities in the mid-winter of global recession).

Such is the level of overinvestment that it has been revealed that in the border region near Mongolia, there is a brand new city for 1m inhabitants that stands empty because there is a perfectly fine, older version just down the road where most citizens prefer to stay!

Of course, the SOEs also expanded production. In steel, for instance, China now has more steel capacity than the rest of the world put together and produces 12 times more than the US — an economy three times bigger than China's. The same over-capacity is found in cement and aluminium: China produces ten times as much cement as the US and five times as much aluminium, with greater production per capita in steel and cement. The Chinese economy is now more concentrated in manufacturing and in investment than any other Asian economy at a similar stage of development (Figure 66).

It is likely that a meaningful proportion of this is malinvestment, characteristic of all bubble economies. China's level of steel capacity and output is not dictated by the amount of steel that it actually needs. It is a function of underpriced capital being made readily available to invest irrespective of returns. Steel producers don't seem to care. They even stockpile dirt (well, iron ore is nearly that). China imported nearly 40% more iron ore per tonne of steel produced in 2009 than 2008 and that can't all be down to us-

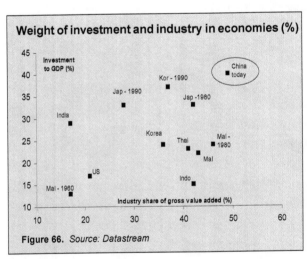

Figure 66. *Source: Datastream*

ing better quality Australian iron ore than their own (Figure 67)!

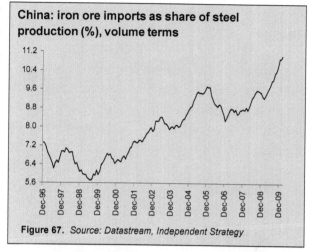

China: iron ore imports as share of steel production (%), volume terms

Figure 67. *Source: Datastream, Independent Strategy*

However, even the SOEs didn't have the capacity to absorb all the lending that needed to be done. So next in line for forced feeding were the Window Companies. These are semi state-owned corporations that are usually controlled by SOEs. Window Companies, from a Chinese banker's point of view, are the next best thing to lend to after a SOE. That's because in China credit quality is measured by how close the satellite company is to the sun of the state — the closer, the better. In reality, of course, the opposite is often true.

Frequently, a Window Company's purpose is to invest in assets. So, given credit, that's what it will do. Whereas the poor, pure SOE has to invest in inventories or boring plant and equipment related to its business, the Window Companies can invest in asset bubbles left, right and centre.

In Hong Kong, a Mainland Window Company will invest in property, almost at any price. This causes the macrocosm of the China credit bubble to spill over into a HK real estate bubble. Because the Window Company's business is to invest in assets, it can get permission to export capital from China to do so in HK property. Once it has bought the HK real estate, it goes to a local HK bank and raises a mortgage. That's when the chips are cashed into foreign currency and god knows what happens to the proceeds next. As it takes a court order to reveal the real owner of property in HK, Window Companies provide an excellent way to hide the identities of mainland investors — even from their own authorities — and encourage speculation.

The property sits on the Window Company's books along with the HK mortgage as well as the original Chinese bank loan and both borrowings are serviced by it. The HK real estate asset has been leveraged twice: once by the Window Company and again through the HK mortgage. The price paid for the HK property or what happens to its market value is irrelevant; it is just a chip to be cashed. The real money gain is simply the cash from leveraging the asset, which may, of course, instantaneously disappear from sight.

The Beijing authorities are now trying to clamp down on these excesses. The trouble is that bubbles don't usually deflate gently, they burst. You can control the timing to a limited degree, but not the consequences. If the commercial banks can no longer lend without increasing deposits, new lending will stall fast. Whereas bank deposits were growing at an annualised rate of over 40% this time last year, deposit growth has now slowed to a single-digit rate. The official loan-deposit ratio remains under the 75% limit set by the Chinese Banking Regulatory Commission (Figure 68). But there is little room for expanding loans from here. The authorities have ordered banks to cut new lending in 2010 to Rmb7trn from nearly Rmb10trn in 2009.

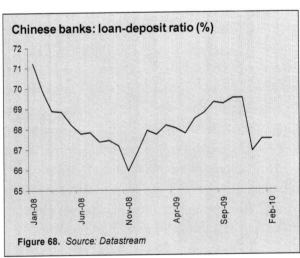

Figure 68. *Source: Datastream*

Why is China's credit bubble part of the global sovereign debt crisis? After all, isn't China's public debt ratio pretty low by international standards? Maybe it is, at least on the official data. But the huge fiscal and monetary stimulus of 2009 now sits on top of the existing official public sector debt, which is officially put at nearly 20% of GDP. China's official debt to GDP figure excludes loans by policy banks and bad debts in state-owned asset management corporations.

Above all, the official debt figure excludes loans incurred by local governments in China through their Local Government Financing Vehicles (LGFVs). The latter have borrowed massively to build infrastructure. Borrowing by LGFVs between 2004 and the end of 2009 reached about $1.6trn (Rmb11trn), or roughly one-third of China's 2009 GDP and 70% of its foreign-exchange reserves. So on top of the official debt, there is an additional 30% of GDP in gross borrowing. Then there are the central government guarantees, such as the nearly Rmb1trn (equal to 3% of GDP) in railway bonds and bonds issued by the asset management companies. So China's public debt ratio is much higher than the official figure — probably north of 70% of GDP (Figure 69).

Should China experience a credit crunch, that will have international implications. Not only will global growth be hit, but the funding of government deficits in the US, the UK and even Japan will be that much more difficult if China stops buying their bonds.

That could happen if the bursting credit bubble encouraged the Chinese administration to turn more of their foreign currency holdings into renminbi to use as stimulus at home. This would be highly inflationary because the foreign currency holdings of China have already been converted into domestic currency and used, which is why the foreign currency ended up in China's international reserves in the first place.

China's credit bubble is unique because it is highly domesticated. That makes timing of its demise impossible to gauge. But a credit bubble is a credit bubble and that makes China part of the global sovereign debt problem, not a solution to it. The misallocation of resources that credit bubbles cause will have a real economic cost that China cannot avoid.

China's off-balance sheet public debt

The rot on the borrowing side of China's credit explosion is located in Local Government Financing Vehicles (LGFVs) belonging to one of China's many levels of local government ranging from towns, counties, to cities and provinces. LGFVs are conduits, like SIVs were for western banks, which are used by local government to borrow and spend on infrastructure and other projects (like real estate). The local government owners inject cash and land banks into the LGFV to give it assets and a capital base for borrowing, as well as subsidising their debt servicing. Guarantees of LGFV debt by local government are also common (as are guarantees of one LGFV's debts by another).

The usefulness of the LGFV is that it allows the local government to borrow and spend way in excess of its own budget, where normally tax revenues cover only about half expenditure (with the rest coming from Beijing). There are over 8000 LGFVs in China with only paltry information available for all but 100 of them and even for those the information is incomplete. LGFVs are used to divert funds borrowed for authorized projects to other ends (e.g. loans for infrastructure spending channelled into real estate speculation by local cadres) or to borrow and feed back the proceeds to local government. They are predominantly unprofitable with debt service on existing debts funded by further cash subsidies from local government and other borrowings. Asset injections can be at inflated prices to dress up balance sheets and facilitate borrowing. Many LGFVs are insolvent.

According to a study by Professor Shih of Northwestern University, the total borrowings of LGFVs are RMB11trn, which we would break down roughly into RMB7trn borrowed for infrastructure spending and RMB4trn for "other" purposes. LGFV borrowings account for approximately one-third of GDP, 25% of outstanding RMB bank credit and more than 80% of new bank loans during the 2009 credit bubble. Inclusion of LGFV debt (and other unconsolidated forms of state credit) in total government debt would lift China's gross sovereign debt to GDP ratio to 60-70%, at the level at which Rogoff and Reinhart estimate that emerging market average GDP growth rates would fall by 2% pts below trend. A 30% loss-given default ratio on a non-performing loan ratio of 30% on Professor Shih's loan estimates would cost China nearly 3% of GDP and 25% of its bank equity.

China: public sector debt estimates (% of GDP)

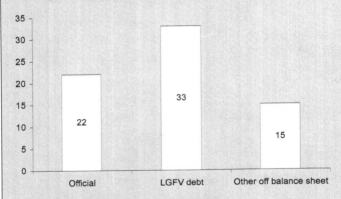

Figure 69. Source: Victor Shih, Independent Strategy

CHAPTER TEN

The winners and losers

As we have seen in previous chapters, the sovereign debt burdens of nearly all major governments are burgeoning. In the case of the most vulnerable OECD countries and many emerging markets, budget deficits cannot be funded domestically because of a dearth of domestic savings. The US, the UK and Japan are the most vulnerable of the larger economies in the OECD (see Appendix for our Sovereign Debt Vulnerability Index).

The governments of these economies will all have to feed from the same trough of international savings. Supply and demand will push up bond yields, making the stock of sovereign debt much less affordable. Any attempt by governments to inflate away their debts will simply make them more costly and reduce growth further. The impact of the rising cost of sovereign debt on budget arithmetic will be rapid because the duration of government debt is generally short (except for the UK).

The stock of sovereign debt is likely to continue to grow faster than GDP. This is because sovereign interest rates will rise and remain above nominal GDP growth. To stop the debt spiral would take a swing in fiscal tightening (measured by the required improvement in the annual primary budget balance) of 8-10% of GDP or more in the US, the UK and Japan.

Once excessive debt and deficit policies have kicked off, they are self-feeding (particularly if interest rates are higher than growth — as they almost always are in a post-bubble world). The debt burdens of deficit-ridden governments are now growing exponentially. Levels of sovereign debt in most OECD countries will reach 70-120% of GDP by 2011, up by 50-150% from before the crisis.

Post-crisis economic growth will provide little help in reducing the sovereign debt burden. It will be hampered by the use of policies to fight the credit crisis that prolong excesses and thus damage future productivity.

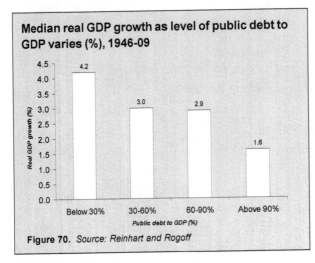

Median real GDP growth as level of public debt to GDP varies (%), 1946-09

Figure 70. Source: Reinhart and Rogoff

As we have seen, there is a tipping point for sovereign debt to GDP leverage when the Keynesian medicine stops working — even as a temporary fix (and it was never meant to be anything else).

At somewhere between 60-100% of GDP, increased government debt reduces GDP growth rather than adds to it (Figure 70). The reason is primarily the Ricardian effect: namely, people and corporations save to pay the future taxes and reduction in government benefits that deficit spending ultimately entails.

The hints of a sovereign debt crisis spooking markets make last year's stimulus an unrepeatable act. The fact that key programmes used to finance sovereign leverage are running out of steam is another factor.

We have used Japan as a neat example of these vulnerabilities. The average maturity of Japanese government debt is among the shortest in the OECD. Yet the yield on its long-term JGBs remains very low for a government that is running out of savings to fund the largest stock of government debt and one of the biggest fiscal deficits (measured as a proportion of GDP) in the OECD.

If Japan had to borrow internationally at the same rate as fiscally-prudent Germany, the cost of servicing its debt would rise from 3% to 8% of GDP. This would increase its already unsustainable budget deficit by 50% (Figure 71).

This risk of the increasing cost of sovereign debt will push nearly all governments to try and lock in current low bond yields by borrowing longer term. However, this also means that investors will have to make a long-term forecast of the solvency of governments whose debt they buy. They will have to price in the increasing likelihood of crisis or insolvency and any future attempts to inflate away sovereign debt burdens. This will contribute to increasing the cost of borrowing to governments. (For the technically-minded: the term premium will rise from currently abnormally low levels).

Government bond ratings will increasingly come under threat. The poor fiscal fundamentals of the US, Japan, the UK, France and other European states require firm fiscal consolidation quickly or there is the risk of derating. Indeed, the continued use of developed countries' government bond yields as the risk-free rate will be placed in jeopardy.

All this heralds a higher global cost of capital and weak economic growth, at best. But it could be worse. There is increasing risk of a series of sovereign debt defaults. In our chapter on Europe, we highlighted the danger signals with the crisis over Greek sovereign debt, which could conceivably spread to the other big-deficit/high-debt economies in the Eurozone and, by contagion, the Eastern European states. But even if the EU is successful in drawing a line in the sand around euro members, the sovereign debt crisis can quickly migrate elsewhere.

Despite the prevailing view that emerging markets are immune to the credit crisis, they

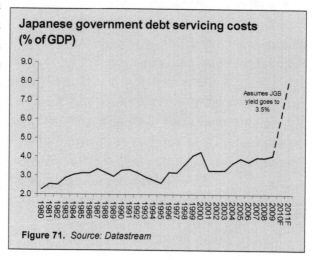

Figure 71. *Source: Datastream*

can suffer from a greater dearth of foreign buyers at (admittedly) lower levels of sovereign debt. They lack deep, liquid domestic debt markets. Consequently, the threshold for sovereign debt crises in emerging markets is lower than for developed economies. And the growth assumptions that underpin optimism about their ability to service their debts are vulnerable to disappointing exports due to low growth in their rich crisis-struck trading partners, as well as from the bursting of the China bubble.

If all this is clear to us, why is it not so to markets? Despite exploding government debt, sovereign bond yields are near all-time lows. The market view is that the driver of bond yields is inflation. And this, it believes, will stay low, due to the paltry nature of economic recovery and the existence of large output gaps in terms of both spare capacity and labour.

But much of the so-called output gap includes malinvestment in capacity, built up during the bubble economy, which will never be used again (e.g. US construction equipment). Worse, measures of the output gap are subject to such wild and prolonged historical revisions as to make them useless as a measure of current economic slack.

Much the same logic applies to the skills of people previously employed in the bubble sectors. Their skill sets may make it hard to re-deploy such people rapidly into recovery sectors (e.g. real estate agents have problems becoming silicone chip processors and investment bankers make poor shoe-shine boys). People who are *un*-employable do not hold down the wages of those who are employable for very long.

And there's another factor: big government! Inflation may be low now, but big government and rising sovereign debt and deficits represent a misallocation of resources that will generate inflation down the road. Big government does so because the low productivity and market meddling of enlarged bureaucracies always lead to lower productivity and growth and higher inflation. Big deficits guarantee the allocation of savings to low productivity uses. It's just a matter of time.

The consensus is that the dreaded fat-tail risks in the probability curve of outcomes have been shrinking. But the economic recovery is being built on excessive, increased leverage (the cause of the credit crisis in the first place) and an unprecedented expansion of central bank balance sheets. We doubt that this is the basis for stability. All that has changed is that government and central bank leverage is being piled on top of minimal deleveraging by the private sector.

Back in the darkest hours of the credit crisis, we argued that it would take years to reduce leverage and the global economy would stumble on slowly on the basis of a return to thrift and productive investment. The dire outcome of outright debt deflation would be avoided, but not the pain of past excesses.

But that was before everything was done to ensure that over-leverage would be maintained, market-clearing prices for bubble assets would be prevented from working their cure and double-digit percentages of GDP were thrown into the pot as fiscal stimulus and central bank liquidity injections.

The picture has changed and the fat-tail risks have grown (Figure 72). A 'dead duck' scenario (40% probability) of a long, painful workout spanning five to six years is our central thesis. But the risks of the outliers — a boomlet followed by a new bust or a near-term collapse back into recession — have increased.

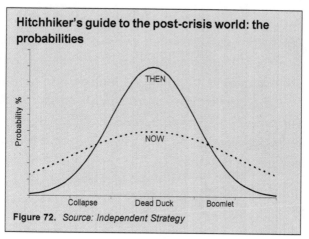

Figure 72. *Source: Independent Strategy*

This heightened uncertainty is directly the result of two things: the size of the resources employed to reflate a bubble economy and the enthusiastic reaction of financial markets to them.

A 'collapse' scenario (25% probability) is predicated upon the argument that the size of fiscal and monetary stimulus is unrepeatable and unsustainable, but responsible for 100% of current economic growth. So growth will fade as stimulus wanes. Under this scenario, sovereign bond yields would initially gap up 100-200 basis points due to supply/demand imbalances; while equities would collapse 50-60% as growth tanks. Credit problems buried in the current financial asset boom would resurface with a vengeance. But there would be no effective policy tools left to fight the Great Deflation. Of course, that doesn't mean the politicians and central bankers wouldn't try. In the longer term, there would be mass printing of money and the monetisation of government debt. Competitive devaluations as well as trade and capital restrictions would be the new policy tools, heralding a return to the 'national economy'. Indeed, one possible outcome is that so much money gets printed, the 'collapse' merges into a stagflationary environment. But more likely, in the longer-term stage of the collapse scenario, sovereign bonds would perform as deflation deepened and central banks monetised debt; while equities, having collapsed, would stay down.

An alternative fat tail scenario is 'boom and bust' (35% probability). This scenario is based upon the authorities being successful in igniting a two-year economic boom, using leverage to do so. Jobs would do the V–shaped thing. Credit would recover. Households in the thriftless Anglo-Saxon economies would shop until they dropped. The next bust wouldn't take too long to happen, because the boomlet would jack up interest rates, reflecting plummeting savings and increased borrowing, as well as renewed inflation.

THE WINNERS AND LOSERS

The boomlet would become a bust because its fuel is leverage. The US current account deficit would widen while the boom lasted. That would add to downward pressure on the dollar and upward pressure on US interest rates, because overseas investors would be reluctant to finance it. Bond yields would rise 400-600 basis points. Even the world's most profligate central banks would be forced to tighten. The boomlet economy would initially boost equities. But they would soon be capped by accelerating inflation and rising interest rates.

The idea that equities are a hedge against inflation can only be entertained by those who didn't live through (or study) the 1970s. They can only be a hedge against inflation if profits rise faster than prices. That can only happen if increases in input prices constantly lag output prices — and that's impossible. The ensuing bust would herald debt deflation. At this point, the scenario rejoins that of the collapse scenario, with the prices of equities, energy and commodities collapsing. Then the same policies as under that scenario would be employed, leading to the outperformance of sovereign debt and little else.

But our central case remains the 'dead duck' scenario (Figure 73). Under this scenario, trend OECD growth falls to 1-2% a year as fiscal handouts fade, household deleveraging continues and any recovery in the jobs

Hitchhiker's guide to the post-crisis world: the consequences		
Collapse (25%)	**Dead duck central case (40%)**	**Boomlet and bust (35%)**
Near term (1-2 years)	_Near term (1-2 years)_	_Near term (1-2 years)_
Fiscal deficits widen	Low growth	Fast growth
Sovereign debt crises	Inflation creeps up	Credit and consumer boom
Protectionism	Fiscal deficits and debts stay high	Global imbalances worsen
	Sovereign yields double	Sovereign yields treble
Longer-term (3-5 years)	_Longer-term (3-5 years)_	_Longer-term (3-5 years)_
Deflation	Shift to thrift	High inflation and yields
Monetisation of debt and	Low productivity	Credit dives
deficits	Move to consumer economy in EMs	New debt inflation

Figure 73. _Source: Independent Strategy_

market is paltry. Productivity falls victim to big government and the legacy problems of the credit crisis. Governments go on spending, but not enough to produce a bubble boom. Nevertheless, their fiscal deficits and debts remain too high and sovereign bond yields are on a rising trend.

Under this scenario, the global economy is likely to return to low, positive growth with high, single-digit inflation and low productivity gains. Economic performance will be weighed down by the legacy of leverage and malinvestment; the shift to thrift by households; and the damage inflicted by big government on market mechanisms (increased bureaucracy, regulation, market meddling, and the crowding-out of productive investment by public debt burdens).

Low growth and poor job figures are likely to produce grinding protectionism, but not on a scale that would cancel globalisation, result in global deflation or a return to the 'national' economy.

By our reckoning, this central Dead Duck thesis still has more chance of happening than the fat tails of collapse or boomlet and bust. But at 40%, that probability is below the comfort level of 50%. So weighting the outcomes doesn't help you invest: as Heinrich Boehl wrote, if you are bitten by a snake, you have only a 10% chance of dying, but if you do, you are 100% dead.

Another feature of the last decade that led up to the financial crisis was global imbalances. Excess leverage and inadequate thrift produced unsustainable current account deficits in many OECD countries. The credit bubble was the means of financing this. We exposed this in our earlier book, *New Monetarism*, at a time when we were being told by Ben Bernanke at the Federal Reserve that global imbalances were in a sustainable, if sub-optimal, equilibrium — a product of a 'global savings glut' caused by excessive saving in Asia, especially China.

At the time, we refuted that argument, showing that *net* savings rose in Asia, not because of rising gross savings (which did not rise much) but because of falling investment. The US external imbalance was not caused by factors outside the US but by excessive borrowing inside the country. Now recent research has confirmed that view — namely that the causality runs from a credit-fuelled asset bubble to a current account deficit[1].

Under the Dead Duck scenario, these global imbalances would reverse gradually in a positive fashion. The boomlet scenario would make them worse temporarily. So US interest rates would soar and the dollar would slide.

The collapse scenario would reduce the US current account deficit but in a way that would spread the pain of deflation to its trading partners in a disorderly way, resulting in 'beggar-thy-neighbour' protectionism and competitive devaluations of trading partner currencies, particularly in Asia.

So, for us, the impact of the sovereign debt explosion is at odds with the sanguine consensus view. For the consensus, global economic recovery will be moderate, but enough to solve all the legacy problems of the credit crisis. Emerging markets will happily replace the tired old OECD economies as drivers of global GDP, due to vibrant domestic growth. Inflation will stay low because output gaps are large. Profit growth will match world economic recovery, allowing equity markets to rise. Central banks will tighten a little but not too much, so asset prices will be supported. Credit growth will resume as household incomes recover. The dollar will appreciate because the US economy, having adopted all the right policies, will be the first to recover. And of course, the US is 'the greatest free market economy in the world', so it deserves to do so.

An awful lot of things have to go right for such a happy outcome. We doubt that they will. But the fundamental difference in the consensus analysis is that it ignores the kernel issue that we seek to address — for right or wrong. That is that every economic up-cycle in the last 25 years, including the one currently predicted by financial markets, has been

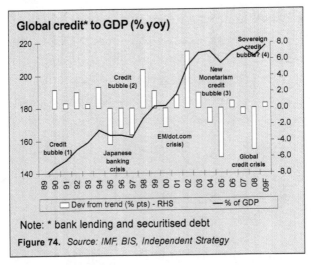

Global credit* to GDP (% yoy)

Note: * bank lending and securitised debt

Figure 74. *Source: IMF, BIS, Independent Strategy*

achieved by massive expansion of credit and leverage with ensuing asset bubbles (Figure 74). Can we generate another such cycle? If not, what will generate growth?

Much more likely, we are just at the beginning of a global sovereign debt crisis that will, at best, keep global economic growth below pre-crisis trend levels and at worst lead to a series of debt defaults.

Investment — what to do?

What should investors do? As we showed earlier, according to history, global sovereign debt crises happen in waves of defaults. We could be about to have a tsunami. So don't buy sovereign debt before it is distressed a lot more. Debt-sick governments may resort to imposing compulsory purchases of their debt on pension funds and financial institutions as liquid buffers of 'safe' assets. So once central banks have 'normalised' policy rates, investors should bet again on rising government bond yields.

Equities will be losers from sovereign bond repricing on three fronts. First, the so-called risk-free government bond yield will rise, reducing ex ante equity risk premiums. Second, economic growth will be slower than anticipated, reducing profit growth. And third, higher inflation will reduce the present value of distant earnings.

Global equities are unattractive at current prices (Figure 75). Emerging market equities are likely to disappoint even more because of the end of the China bubble, weak commodity prices and, in Eastern Europe, the renewed risk of a foreign debt crisis.

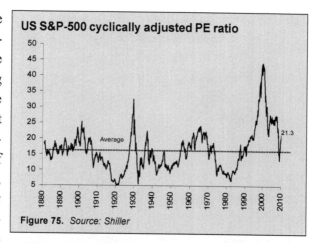

Figure 75. *Source: Shiller*

There could be a crossover of yields between government and blue-chip corporate debt (Figure 76). Inflation affects both equally, which boils the issue down to

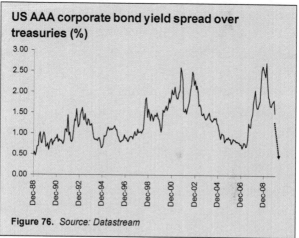

Figure 76. *Source: Datastream*

credit quality. Markets would prevent governments creating enough monetary-induced inflation to reduce their real debt burdens significantly. And governments have less ability to raise more revenue by increasing taxes than well-run corporations do with decent products.

Bond markets are already beginning to reflect this tectonic change. For example, it is now safer to lend to Warren Buffett than Barack Obama. Two-year notes sold by Berkshire Hathaway now yield 3.5 basis points less than US treasuries of similar maturity.

The US government will spend more on debt service as a percentage of revenue this year (11%) than any other top-rated country except the UK.

Banks will be regulated like utilities. The amount of low return capital they will have to set aside as insurance for their risk assets will lower profitability. And they are in the cross hairs of financial repression by being obliged to invest in sovereign debt.

The euro will be weak for a while due to the sovereign debt crisis in the distressed peripheral Eurozone economies. But under German tutelage, the Eurozone will eventually become the most conservatively-managed fiscal and monetary region in the world and the euro will become strong again, as a result. Eastern European debt and currencies will be affected by the delay imposed upon those countries in trying to join the euro, which amplifies the risk of their over-exposure to foreign-currency debt.

The only way for Japan to bring its sovereign debt down to a manageable level is to monetise it, run a much weaker currency and tolerate higher inflation. Barring that outcome, Japan's sovereign debt will ultimatley have to be restructured.

Ultimately, the dollar will suffer from US policies of denial and the absence of any savings cushion to help the economy adjust to an unleveraged growth path. When the markets wake up to this, the dollar will resume its decade of decline.

Gold will remain a safe haven asset in this time of prolonged sovereign debt crisis and policy attempts to inflate away debt burdens. But other commodities, as well as resource-based currencies like the Aussie and Kiwi dollars, could be natural-born victims of the collapse of the China credit bubble and reduced Asian regional growth, at least for a time.

Silver linings

There are some silver linings in this sovereign debt crisis. First, there is Europe. Germany is in the process of taking control of ECB monetary policy and Eurozone fiscal policy. It will apply the Maastricht criteria strictly throughout the Eurozone. Germany has enshrined strict fiscal orthodoxy in its own constitution as an exit strategy from the exceptional policy measures it enacted to deal with the credit crisis.

EU-wide compliance with the Maastricht criteria can only be achieved through smaller government. There is no way that taxes can be raised significantly in Europe as government is already too big and taxes too high. Reducing the size of government will bring the biggest dividends: each euro of decreased government may result in two euros of extra GDP and wealth expansion as entrepreneurs step up to the plate vacated by government.

Japan will experience a public debt crisis. But this crisis may have a silver lining, if it becomes a wake-up call for politicians to empower domestic consumption, bring women into the workforce, reform the tax base (particularly inheritance tax) and promote immigration. The gender gap between men and women participating in the full-time labour force and discrimination in pay is the largest in the G7 (Figure 77). Integrating women into the Japanese workforce has the potential to raise GDP by 15-20%.

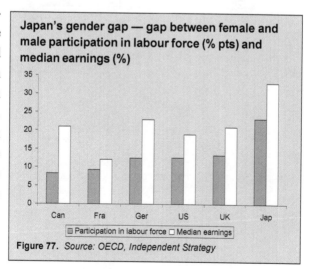

Figure 77. *Source: OECD, Independent Strategy*

All of these measures could reinvigorate the way Japan Inc makes things rather than what it makes (which is already superb). It's a lot easier to make a factory more productive that has great products than one that produces things no one wants.

A Chinese credit crisis could produce a positive outcome if the shock makes China serious about developing a domestic consumer economy rather than a manufacturing and export-driven one. That's a decade-long project whose time has come from the standpoint of the wealth and income levels per capita of a sufficient swathe of the population.

To let it happen, wages have to rise by around 15% of national income, growth will have to be driven by services on the supply side and consumption on the demand side of the economy (Figure 78). Moreover, the social and political aspirations of a burgeoning middle class have to be matched by political reform. That's a tough task for the ex-Communist elite.

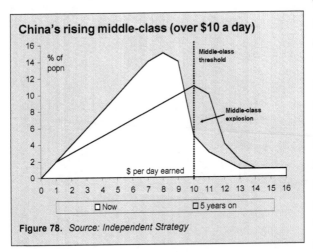

Figure 78. *Source: Independent Strategy*

1. *Capital Flows, Consumption Booms and Asset Bubbles: a behavioural alternative to the savings glut hypothesis*, Economic Journal, Laibson, David and Johanna Mollerstrom, March 2010

Sovereign debt vulnerability index

Which advanced economies are most vulnerable to a sovereign debt crisis? In our sovereign debt vulnerability index, we have identified seven key variables to gauge that vulnerability for the main OECD economies. They are: 1) the level of gross public sector debt forecast for 2011; 2) the rate of expansion in gross public debt from 2007 to 2011; 3) the cyclically-adjusted primary budget balance; 4) the basic balance of payments (i.e. current account plus net foreign direct investment and portfolio flows; 5) the domestic national savings rate 6) the share of foreign ownership of outstanding government debt; and 7) the annual rollover rate for government debt redemptions.

The gross public debt measure accounts for the sheer size of the debt problem. The expansion of debt in the credit crisis measures the impact of the crisis on government finances. The structural primary budget balance measure shows how government policies on taxes and spending are geared to curb any rise in debt, excluding any cyclical effect from economic growth, inflation or 'automatic stabilisers'.

The remaining measures seek to gauge the strength or weakness in the 'domestication' of the funding of sovereign debt The basic balance of payments measures the ability of an economy to raise extra resources to service government debt from abroad. The domestic savings rate is a key measure of the domestic resources available to finance public spending and debt while supporting investment and economic growth. The foreign ownership of debt measure reveals the vulnerability of a government to the loss of confidence by foreign investors. And the rollover rate measures the timing and pressure on debt redemptions.

We set thresholds for each measure to pinpoint trigger points for vulnerability, giving scores when the thresholds were reached. Also we weighted those scores according to certain thresholds reached. We gave the highest weightings to the level of debt, the primary balance, the national savings rate and foreign ownership of government debt.

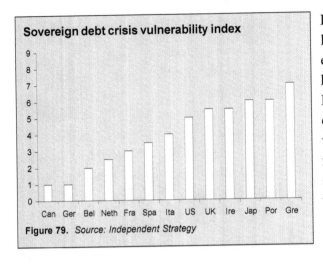

Sovereign debt crisis vulnerability index

Figure 79. *Source: Independent Strategy*

In this way, we looked at the G7 economies plus the key countries in the Eurozone and came up with a vulnerability score for each country's sovereign debt, which are outlined in Figure 79. Not surprisngly, Greece and Portugal were the most vulnerable to a debt crisis on our index. But Japan also finished near the top, with Ireland and the UK just behind. The US also scored above the mid-point for vulnerability. Canada and Germany were the least vulnerable, while France, Spain and Italy were below the mid-point.

The raw data and our weightings are provided in Figure 80.

Sovereign debt variables

	A	B	C	D	E	F	G
Belgium	105	20	-2	19	22	48	19
Canada	79	0	-3	3	19	15	7
France	83	24	-7	7	18	52	12
Germany	80	15	-4	2	19	46	14
Greece	135	40	-6	1	7	70	18
Ireland	96	71	-8	-18	17	62	14
Italy	120	14	-3	4	15	41	17
Japan	227	44	-7	-8	23	7	42
Netherlands	70	24	-4	11	25	58	13
Portugal	91	28	-6	-7	10	72	14
Spain	74	38	-5	-5	20	57	11
UK	91	44	-10	5	12	28	6
US	94	21	-9	-3	13	48	20
Thresholds	>90	>20	<-3	<-3	<15	>25*	>15
	>120	>40	<-5	<-6	<10	>50**	>25
Weight	1.0	0.5	1.0	0.5	1.0	1.0	0.5
	1.5	1.0	1.5	1.0	1.5	1.5	1.0
Scores							
Belgium	1.0	0.5	0.0	0.0	0.0	0.0	0.5
Canada	0.0	0.0	1.0	0.0	0.0	0.0	0.0
France	0.0	0.5	1.5	0.0	0.0	1.0	0.0
Germany	0.0	0.0	1.0	0.0	0.0	0.0	0.0
Greece	1.5	1.0	1.5	0.0	1.5	1.0	0.5
Ireland	1.0	1.0	1.5	1.0	0.0	1.0	0.0
Italy	1.5	0.0	1.0	0.0	1.0	0.0	0.5
Japan	1.5	1.0	1.5	1.0	0.0	0.0	1.0
Netherlands	0.0	0.5	1.0	0.0	0.0	1.0	0.0
Portugal	1.0	0.5	1.5	1.0	1.0	1.0	0.0
Spain	0.0	0.5	1.5	0.5	0.0	1.0	0.0
UK	1.0	1.0	1.5	0.0	1.0	1.0	0.0
US	1.0	0.5	1.5	0.5	1.0	0.0	0.5

Key:
A = Sovereign debt/GDP
B = % change in sovereign debt , 2007-11
C = Primary structural budget balance, 2009 (% of GDP)
D = Basic balance of payments (% of GDP, 2009)
E = Domestic national savings/GDP, 2009
F = Foreign ownership of sovereign debt (% share)
G = Required rollover rate (% p.a.)

Note:
*Eurozone countries must score under 50%, non-Eurozone must score under 25%.
**The US need score under 50% to compensate for the role of the US$ as reserve currency.

Figure 80. Source: Independent Strategy

Bibliography

Y Altanbus, L Gambacorta, D Marques-Ibanez, *Does monetary policy affect bank risk-taking?*, BIS working paper 298, March 2010

T Adrian, HS Shin, *The changing nature of financial intermediation and the financial crisis of 2007-09*, New York Fed staff report No 439, March 2010

S Berkman, G Gelos, R Rennhack, JP Walsh, *The global financial crisis: Were some countries hit harder?*, IMF research, March 2010

H Blommertein and A Glock, *The surge in borrowing needs of OECD governments 2009-10*, OECD Financial Market Trends, December 2009

C Borio and P Low, *Asset prices, financial and monetary stability: exploring the nexus*, BIS working paper, No 114, July 2002

M Bordo, *When bubbles burst*, IMF WEO, April 2003

L Cappiello, A Kadareja, CK Sorenson, M Protopapa, *Do bank loans and credit have an effect on output?*, ECB working paper 1150, January 2010

A Cebotari, *Contingent liabilities: issues and practice,* IMF working paper, 245, 2008

S Cechetti, M Mohanty, F Zampolli, *The future of public debt: prospects and implications*, BIS working paper, February 2010

B Coulton, *High grade and Euro area sovereign risk*, Fitch Ratings, March 2010

BIBLIOGRAPHY

J Gohale, *Measuring unfunded obligations of European countries,* NCPA, January 2009

Alan Greenspan, *The crisis*, Greenspan Associates, March 2010

A Mody, F Ohnsorge, *After the crisis*, IMF working paper 1011, January 2010

C Reinhart and K Rogoff, *The forgotten history of domestic debt*, April 2008

C Reinhart, K Rogoff, *This time is different: a panoramic view of eight centuries of financial crises*, April 2008

C Reinhart, K Rogoff, *Growth in a time of debt*, January 2010

M Roberts *The Great Recession,* November 2009

D Roche, R McKee, *New Monetarism*, 2nd edition, September 2008

C Roxburgh, S Lund, T Wimmer, *Debt and deleveraging: the global debt bubble and its economic consequences*, January 2010

V Shih, *The looming problems of local debt in China*, Northwestern University, February 2010